SAUCES
& SALSAS

SAUCES & SALSAS

Oded Schwartz

Photography by Ian O'Leary

DORLING KINDERSLEY
London • New York • Sydney
www.dk.com

A DORLING KINDERSLEY BOOK

Project Editor Nasim Mawji

Art Editor Sue Storey
at Patrick McLeavy & Partners

Senior Editor Jane Middleton

Senior Art Editor Tracey Ward

DTP Designer Bridget Roseberry

Managing Editor Susannah Marriott

Managing Art Editor Toni Kay

Deputy Art Director Carole Ash

Production Controller Sarah Coltman

Food Stylists Alison Austin,
Jane Suthering and Oded Schwartz

*This book is for Vicki McIvor, my agent and my friend.
Without her encouragement, trust and dedication
my work would have been impossible.*

All recipes serve 4–6 unless otherwise indicated

Some recipes in this book contain raw eggs. Because of the
risk of salmonella poisoning, young children, the elderly,
pregnant women and those with impaired immune
systems should avoid raw eggs.

First published in Great Britain in 1999
by Dorling Kindersley Limited
9 Henrietta Street, London WC2E 8PS

www.dk.com

A CIP catalogue record for this book is available from the British Library

ISBN 0 7513 0785 8

Reproduced in Singapore by Colourscan
Printed and bound in Spain by Artes Gráficas Toledo S.A.U.
D.L. TO: 1259 - 1999

CONTENTS

INTRODUCTION

THERE IS NO SORCERY INVOLVED IN MAKING A GOOD SAUCE – all you need are fresh ingredients, simple techniques, a bit of patience and a dash of imagination.

From the simple sauces of ancient civilizations – mixtures of vinegar, salt and oils – to the elegant, rich concoctions of classic French cuisine, sauces have always played an important part in cooking. Recently, though, they have fallen out of favour with home cooks, who tend to think that they are fiddly and time-consuming to prepare as well as being rich and highly calorific. This book takes a new approach and aims to show that sauces can be light, fresh and quick to make. It provides step-by-step advice on classic techniques – for béchamel, hollandaise, beurre blanc, sabayon and coulis, for example – and also includes a huge range of modern sauces and relishes.

In response to our increasingly adventurous palates, our hectic lifestyles and considerably healthier eating habits, here are sauces in the broadest sense of the word. Salsas – combinations of finely chopped fresh fruit and vegetables that require no cooking at all – can enliven a piece of grilled chicken or fish. Fresh dips can be served as part of a mezze or eaten as a light snack. Dressings can be drizzled over a bowl of crisp leaves. Coconut chutney will transform a simple samosa. I have also included an international selection of hearty and warming cooking sauces, many of which can be left to cook slowly and form an integral part of a dish.

Whether it be a rich hollandaise, a spoonful of spicy paste, a knob of flavoured butter, a freshly prepared relish or a zesty marinade, a well-made sauce can elevate simple ingredients to the sublime. Sauces add moisture, flavour, colour and texture to food. They are also very versatile. Many of the intensely flavoured pastes and relishes can be mixed with cream cheese, yogurt or mayonnaise to make delicious dips and dressings, or spooned over pasta, polenta, couscous or rice for a light meal. Plain sauces can be vehicles for many different flavourings if you vary your choice of herbs and spices. Use your imagination and experiment.

Happily, the days when sauces were regarded with suspicion as a means for concealing poor-quality ingredients are long gone. These days sauces are invariably the crowning glory of a dish. A carefully chosen sauce will perfectly complement the ingredients you are serving it with, highlighting and harmonizing flavours without dominating. The trick is to understand the versatility of sauces and to be imaginative in the way that you serve them. I have included a chart at the end of the book (see Matching Sauces with Food, pages 138–40), to help you partner sauces with appropriate ingredients.

Sauces & Salsas is an eclectic collection of my favourite recipes. Rich, spicy, subtle or delicate, time-honoured or created specially for this book, these recipes represent a fascinating culinary trip round the world. Be saucy with your sauces, and use this book as a guide – a blueprint for new ways of cooking. I hope it will inspire you to create your own new and exciting sauces and salsas and that you enjoy using it as much as I have enjoyed writing it.

A GALLERY OF SAUCES

THIS TANTALIZING GALLERY WILL HELP

YOU TURN FRESH AND EXCITING

INGREDIENTS INTO DELICIOUS AND

APPETIZING SAUCES, SALSAS, MARINADES

AND RELISHES. USE THIS INSPIRATIONAL

COLLECTION OF INGREDIENTS AND IDEAS

TO EXPAND YOUR CULINARY REPERTOIRE.

HERBS & THEIR USES

❖ BAY
Used to flavour stocks, sauces and stews; a pungent leaf which should be used, fresh or dried, in small quantities.

❖ ROSEMARY
Essential in Mediterranean cooking; good with meat, fish and vegetables. Use fresh or dried, but dried tends to be bitter and should be used sparingly.

❖ SAGE
Pungent and should only be used in small quantities as the flavour can be overwhelming; there are several varieties, all of which have a real affinity with meat. The leaves have a soft down.

❖ BASIL
Sweet and superbly fragrant, basil is a classic herb to serve with tomatoes. We think of basil as an Italian herb, but in fact it is just as important in Thai cooking.

❖ TARRAGON
A pungent herb with a complex flavour; it has a real affinity with fish and white meat. Important for flavouring vinegar and many sauces.

❖ PARSLEY
A versatile favourite; the flat-leaf variety has a stronger, fresher flavour. Always use fresh.

❖ OREGANO
A favourite Mediterranean herb with a great affinity with tomatoes as well as lamb and chicken. Used both fresh and dry.

❖ DILL
Fresh-tasting and fragrant with a subtle flavour of anise. Use with fish, chicken or vegetables. Always use fresh.

❖ MINT
There are several varieties of this fresh-tasting and highly aromatic herb. Popular in sauces and excellent with lamb, chicken, pulses, vegetables and fruit.

HERB SAUCES

FRESH, FRAGRANT AND FLAVOURSOME, HERBS ARE ESSENTIAL TO GOOD COOKING. HERBS WITH TOUGH LEAVES, SUCH AS THYME, BAY AND ROSEMARY, HAVE A STRONG FLAVOUR AND SHOULD BE USED SPARINGLY OTHERWISE THEY CAN OVERPOWER AND GIVE A BITTER FLAVOUR. LONG, SLOW COOKING CAN ALTER A HERB'S FLAVOUR — ADDING A SMALL AMOUNT OF THE FRESH HERB JUST BEFORE SERVING CAN REVITALIZE IT. TO KEEP HERBS FRESH, SNIP OFF THE DRY ENDS OF THE STEMS AND EITHER STAND IN A JUG OF FRESH WATER OR WRAP THE STEMS IN DAMP KITCHEN PAPER AND STORE IN A PLASTIC BAG IN THE VEGETABLE DRAWER OF THE REFRIGERATOR. IN GENERAL, FRESH HERBS ARE BETTER THAN DRIED FOR SAUCES, BUT DRIED HERBS HAVE THEIR USES, SUCH AS IN SOME MARINADES AND SPICE PASTES.

ROSEMARY OIL
MAIN IMAGE: rosemary-infused oil drizzled over thin slices of smoked halibut makes an elegant hors d'oeuvre. (*See page 70*)

DILL PESTO
TOP: try dill pesto on polenta topped with grilled red pepper, red onion and shavings of Parmesan. (*See page 120*)

GREEN GODDESS DRESSING
MIDDLE: parsley-flecked green goddess dressing is the perfect accompaniment to a juicy fillet steak. (*See page 72*)

MEDITERRANEAN MARINADE
BOTTOM: swordfish steaks absorb the fresh flavours of a zesty, Mediterranean dill and parsley marinade. (*See page 108*)

SPICES & AROMATICS & THEIR USES

✦ **LEMONGRASS**
The thick stem of a wild grass native to Southeast Asia, this has a lemony flavour and a delicious perfumed aroma.

✦ **CINNAMON**
The aromatic bark of a tree; available as quills, bark chips or ground. Used in sweet and savoury cooking.

✦ **CASSIA**
A close relative of cinnamon, although more commonly used in savoury cooking as it is coarser in flavour. Often added to Indian curries.

✦ **VANILLA**
The fragrant pod of a tropical orchid. Fresh pods have a superior flavour to vanilla extract. However, natural vanilla extract is preferable to synthetic vanilla essence.

✦ **KAFFIR LIME LEAVES**
The fragrant leaves of the kaffir lime tree give a distinctive fresh citrus flavour to many Southeast Asian dishes. Used fresh or dried; the fresh leaves freeze well.

✦ **TAMARIND**
The pod of the tamarind tree, this is available in block or ready-to-use paste form. It gives a fruity, sweet-sour flavour, popular in Indian and Southeast Asian cooking.

✦ **GINGER**
This root has been cultivated in tropical Asia for over 3,000 years. Warming and slightly sweet in flavour, it is best used fresh, but is also available dried, ground and pickled.

✦ **GALANGAL**
The highly aromatic rhizome of a tropical plant. Although interchangeable with ginger, galangal has a stronger, more camphorated flavour, much loved in Malay and Thai cooking.

SAUCES USING SPICES & AROMATICS

JUST AS A PAINTER USES COLOUR TO ADD SUBTLE NUANCES, A COOK USES SPICES AND AROMATICS SUCH AS TAMARIND, GINGER AND VANILLA TO INTRODUCE DELICATE FLAVOURS AND AROMAS TO MANY SAUCES. THE RANGE OF SPICES AND AROMATICS POPULARLY USED IS CONSTANTLY EXPANDING AS MORE EXOTIC INGREDIENTS BECOME WIDELY AVAILABLE. AROMATICS SHOULD BE USED SPARINGLY; MANY ARE QUITE BITTER AND CONCENTRATED IN FLAVOUR AND CAN OVERWHELM. BUY SPICES AND AROMATICS IN SMALL QUANTITIES AND STORE IN TIGHTLY CLOSED CONTAINERS — EXPOSURE TO AIR WILL CAUSE THEIR AROMA TO FADE. WHERE POSSIBLE, FREEZE THEM TO CAPTURE THEIR FRESHNESS.

LEMONGRASS BUTTER SAUCE

MAIN IMAGE: juicy morsels of chicken on a lemongrass skewer with a velvety-smooth aromatic butter sauce. (*See page 54*)

TAMARIND DIPPING SAUCE

TOP: tart and fruity and speckled with spring onions and coriander, this light sauce is perfect for dipping delicate filo parcels. (*See page 125*)

SOUTH AFRICAN SOSATIE

MIDDLE: lamb cutlets in a traditional South African sauce with tamarind, lemon leaves and ginger. (*See page 113*)

EXOTIC FRUIT RELISH

BOTTOM: a sweet concoction of pineapple, aromatic ginger and kaffir lime leaves, served with salmon. (*See page 103*)

CHILLIES & THEIR USES

♦ **ANAHEIM (CHILLI VERDE)**
The most common in the US; also known as California Long. Green, but can be red. Mild.

♦ **CASCABEL (JINGLE BELL)**
Deep red in colour; used fresh or dried. Mild.

♦ **BIRD'S EYE (THAI: PRIK KII NOO SUAN)**
Widely used in Asian kitchens. Either green and fresh or dried and bright red. Very hot.

♦ **CAYENNE (HADES HOT)**
Essential in Creole and Cajun cooking; the original component of cayenne pepper. Very hot.

♦ **SANTA FE GRANDE (CARIBE, CALORO OR GOLD SPIKE)**
Yellow, orange or red, and used fresh or dried, whole or powdered. Mild to moderate.

♦ **CHORICERO**
An important ingredient in Spanish chorizo; a big chilli, used both fresh and dried. Mild.

♦ **GUAJILLO**
A Mexican chilli favoured for its delicate flavour and russet-red colouring. Mild.

♦ **FRESNO**
Light green, ripening to cherry red; used fresh. Hot.

♦ **JALAPEÑO/CHIPOTLE**
Chipotles are smoke-dried jalapeños and have a smoky flavour. Hot

♦ **PASILLA**
Called 'little raisin' in Spanish because of its dried, wrinkled pods and raisin-like aroma; used in stews. Mild to moderate.

♦ **HABANERO (SCOTCH BONNET)**
Intensely flavoured; important in Caribbean cooking. Very hot.

♦ **SERRANO**
Green, red or orange; used fresh. Hot.

CHILLI SAUCES

FRESH, DRIED, HOT, SWEET OR MILD, CHILLIES PLAY AN ESSENTIAL ROLE IN THE GLOBAL KITCHEN, ADDING FLAVOUR, TEXTURE AND A BRIGHT, APPETIZING COLOUR TO SAUCES FROM EVERY CONTINENT. LIKE TOMATOES, CHILLIES WERE INTRODUCED TO THE OLD WORLD FROM THE AMERICAS, WHERE THEY GREW WILD. THEY ARE HIGH IN VITAMINS C AND A, AND IN CAPSAICIN, THE SOURCE OF THEIR HEAT. THE HEAT OF A CHILLI VARIES ACCORDING TO THE TYPE USED (SEE LEFT); BROADLY SPEAKING, SMALLER CHILLIES ARE USUALLY HOTTER BUT THIS IS ONLY A GENERAL RULE. SENSITIVITY TO A CHILLI'S HEAT DIFFERS FROM PERSON TO PERSON, SO, WHEN COOKING WITH CHILLIES, EXERCISE SOME CAUTION, GRADUALLY EXPERIMENTING WITH THE MANY TYPES AND BUILDING UP YOUR PERSONAL TOLERANCE LEVEL.

TOMATO & CHILLI SAUCE

MAIN IMAGE: a tangy, chilli-spiked tomato sauce elevates lightly grilled haddock fillet to gourmet status. (*See page 76*)

THAI DIPPING SAUCE

TOP: an Oriental-style sauce laced with thin slices of chilli makes the perfect accompaniment to prawns. (*See page 125*)

HARISSA

MIDDLE: a versatile chilli sauce that adds instant piquancy to soups, stews, sauces – and even mayonnaise. (*See page 103*)

POMEGRANATE SALSA

BOTTOM: chilli, pomegranate seeds and fresh coriander are combined in this vibrantly coloured salsa. (*See page 97*)

TOMATOES & THEIR USES

♦ BEEF TOMATOES
These are large, juicy, firm-fleshed and easy to peel; a versatile tomato suitable for salsas, salads and stuffing.

♦ COLOURED TOMATOES
Yellow, orange, purple and even striped tomatoes are now readily available. Use these when a different colour sauce is needed.

♦ CHERRY TOMATOES
Bite-sized and sweet-fleshed, these tomatoes are delicious fresh or cooked; as with all tomatoes, vine-ripened ones are more flavoursome.

♦ SUN-DRIED TOMATOES
The raisins of the savoury kitchen, these are usually plum tomatoes that have been cured with salt and dried in the sun; available dried (which need soaking in water before use) or preserved in oil. Intensely flavoured, they need only be used in small quantities.

♦ TOMATO PURÉE
A smooth, concentrated purée of sieved cooked tomatoes. Widely used to add colour and enhance the flavour of cooked tomato dishes. Commercially produced and sold in tins and tubes, but it is also easy to prepare at home.

♦ TINNED TOMATOES
A convenient alternative to fresh tomatoes, particularly in winter. When using, drain off the liquid and gently squeeze out any excess moisture. A standard 400g (13oz) tin of tomatoes, drained and squeezed, is the equivalent of 200–250g (7–8oz) fresh tomatoes. Plum tomatoes are most commonly tinned, but cherry tomatoes are also available.

TOMATO SAUCES

TOMATOES MAKE PARTICULARLY GOOD SAUCES, SINCE THEIR JUICY FLESH COOKS DOWN EASILY TO A PULP. THEY WERE BROUGHT TO THE OLD WORLD FROM THE AMERICAS IN THE 16TH CENTURY BUT IT WAS ONLY WHEN THE ITALIANS EMBRACED TOMATOES WITH SUCH ENTHUSIASM IN THE 19TH CENTURY THAT THEY BECAME UNIVERSALLY POPULAR. NOW IT IS IMPOSSIBLE TO IMAGINE EUROPEAN COOKING WITHOUT THEM. THE BEST TOMATOES HAVE A SUPERB AROMA AND A DELICATE SWEET AND TART BALANCE, PERFECT FOR SAUCES AND SALSAS. COOKING CONCENTRATES THEIR FLAVOUR AND, USED RAW, THEY ADD MOISTURE AND FRUITINESS TO MANY DISHES. TOMATOES CONTAIN CAROTENOIDS, PROVEN CANCER FIGHTERS, WHICH GIVE THEM THEIR RED COLOUR. AVOID USING WATERY SALAD TOMATOES.

FRESH TOMATO COULIS

MAIN IMAGE: the perfect filling for a ripe avocado served with crunchy tortilla chips. (*See page 59*)

TOMATO GRAVY

TOP: fresh tomato purée and sun-dried tomatoes add a wonderful tanginess to traditional pan gravy. (*See page 65*)

TWO-TOMATO RELISH

MIDDLE: sweet-fleshed cherry tomatoes and sun-dried tomatoes in a relish that marries well with chicken. (*See page 103*)

TOMATO RAITA

BOTTOM: plum tomatoes and yogurt are partnered in this cooling, fragrant sauce, perfect with a hot curry. (*See page 104*)

DAIRY PRODUCTS & THEIR USES

✦ MILK
Most milk-based sauces benefit from the rich, smooth texture of full-fat milk rather than semi-skimmed.

✦ SINGLE CREAM
Contains 18–20 per cent butter fat. Suitable for pouring but not for whipping.

✦ DOUBLE CREAM
Smooth and rich, with a minimum of 48 per cent fat; the most useful cream in sauce-making. Suitable for whipping.

✦ CRÈME FRAÎCHE
A type of double cream that has been treated with a culture to give a light acidity without sourness.

✦ SOURED CREAM
Contains 16–40 per cent fat; smooth and mildly acidic in flavour. A popular base for dressings and dips.

✦ YOGURT
Milk soured by the addition of bacteria. Contains 3–10 per cent fat. If using in sauces, be careful not to let it boil or it will curdle.

✦ BLUE CHEESES
Cheeses such as gorgonzola, Stilton and Danish blue contain 30–60 per cent fat and add pungency to many sauces.

✦ FRESH WHITE CHEESES
Skimmed-milk curd cheeses are very low in fat; cream cheese contains about 47 per cent fat. They are used mainly as bases for dips and spreads.

✦ HARD & SEMI-HARD CHEESES
Italian Parmesan, pecorino (made from sheep's milk) and Cheddar contain 30–60 per cent fat. Easy to grate, they are the most commonly used cooking cheeses.

✦ BUTTER
Made by churning cream; use a good-quality unsalted variety when cooking. A knob of butter whisked into a finished sauce adds gloss.

DAIRY SAUCES

MILK, CREAM, BUTTER, YOGURT AND CHEESE ARE THE FOUNDATIONS OF MANY CLASSIC AND MODERN SAUCES. WHAT COULD BE SIMPLER THAN A SAUCE OF MELTED BUTTER, SPIKED WITH A FEW DROPS OF LEMON JUICE? OR SMOOTH CREAM OR YOGURT DELICATELY FLAVOURED WITH FRESH HERBS OR SPICES? FULL-CREAM MILK MAKES THE BASIS FOR COMFORTING WHITE SAUCES AND CUSTARDS. CREAM ADDS RICHNESS AND A VELVETY TEXTURE, WHILE SOURED CREAM, CRÈME FRAÎCHE AND YOGURT LEND SMOOTHNESS, FRESHNESS AND A PLEASANT TARTNESS. CHEESE ADDS FLAVOUR AND TEXTURE AND GIVES AN APPETIZING GOLDEN CRUST TO GRATIN DISHES; BLUE CHEESE LENDS AN UNUSUAL PIQUANCY TO DRESSINGS AND SAUCES. FOR THE BEST FLAVOUR, BUY THE BEST QUALITY CHEESE YOU CAN FIND.

TANDOORI MARINADE

MAIN IMAGE: tandoori poussin and naan. Yogurt in the marinade lends subtlety to the delicate flavours. (*See page 110*)

YOGURT & HONEY SAUCE

TOP: succulent figs with honey-marbled Greek-style yogurt and fresh mint make a light and healthy dessert. (*See page 128*)

CHOCOLATE CUSTARD

MIDDLE: a caramelized orange topped with curls of zest sits in a puddle of rich, smooth chocolate custard. (*See page 126*)

MORNAY SAUCE

BOTTOM: broccoli in a cheese Mornay sauce, lightly grilled to give a slightly crunchy, golden topping. (*See page 49*)

FRUIT & ITS USES

◆ APPLES
For sauce-making use tart cooking apples such as Bramley, which cook down to a smooth pulp. Eating apples, such as Granny Smith, are better diced and used raw in salsas and relishes.

◆ BERRIES
Sweet and sour in flavour, berries cook well and make attractive, brightly coloured sauces. Redcurrants are used in Cumberland sauce; cranberry sauce is the traditional accompaniment to roast turkey.

◆ FRUIT WITH STONES
Ripe cherries, plums, peaches and nectarines make good bases for sweet and savoury sauces. They bruise easily when ripe.

◆ CITRUS FRUITS
Lemons, limes and oranges add tangy flavour. Enhance the citrus flavour in sauces by adding grated zest from unwaxed fruit. The juice of lemons and limes contains vitamin C which helps prevent avocados and some fruits discolouring.

◆ TROPICAL FRUITS
Enzymes in papayas tenderize tough meat; mangoes are delicious in salsas and chutneys; pineapples are popular in chutneys and are also used in meat-tenderizing marinades. Popular for adding exotic flavours – especially to dessert sauces.

◆ BANANAS
Sprinkling with lemon or lime juice prevents discoloration once peeled. Starchy and high in potassium, they are used to thicken and add flavour to many Mexican, Southeast Asian and Indian sauces.

◆ POMEGRANATES
One of the most ancient fruits, indigenous to Persia; edible seeds are encased in juicy, red flesh. A popular ingredient in Middle Eastern cooking; also good in salsas.

FRUIT SAUCES

IT IS VERY EASY TO MAKE SAUCES FROM FRUIT, ESPECIALLY SOFT FRUIT SUCH AS BERRIES, CHERRIES, PLUMS, PEACHES AND MANGOES, WHICH REQUIRE LITTLE OR NO COOKING. RAW, THEY ARE IDEAL FOR QUICK, FRESH-TASTING COULIS AND DESSERT SAUCES; COOKED, THEY CAN BE SERVED WITH SWEET OR SAVOURY FOODS. COOKED SAUCES MADE WITH TART FRUIT SUCH AS APPLES AND PLUMS ARE TRADITIONAL ACCOMPANIMENTS TO ROAST MEAT AND POULTRY. THEY ARE PARTICULARLY GOOD SERVED WITH FATTY MEATS SUCH AS DUCK AND PORK AND OILY FISH SUCH AS MACKEREL TO CUT THE RICHNESS. WITH THEIR FRESH FLAVOUR, CITRUS FRUITS ARE A UNIVERSALLY POPULAR WAY OF ENLIVENING SAUCES. UNLESS YOU PLAN TO USE IT IMMEDIATELY, BUY PRODUCE THAT IS SLIGHTLY UNDERRIPE AND RIPEN IT AT HOME IN YOUR FRUIT BOWL.

BANANA CARAMEL SAUCE
MAIN IMAGE: a rich and luxurious blend of bananas, fresh cream and caramel poured over a tower of hot pancakes. (*See page 129*)

BEETROOT & APPLE SALSA
TOP: creamy goat's cheese on a croûte base with a tangy beetroot and apple salsa and a scattering of red chard. (*See page 96*)

CHERRY SAUCE
MIDDLE: try tart and fresh cherry sauce spooned over a slice of ham and lightly sautéed potatoes. (*See page 118*)

RASPBERRY VINAIGRETTE
BOTTOM: juicy slices of duck on a bed of mixed leaves drizzled with ruby-coloured fresh raspberry vinaigrette. (*See page 69*)

ALCOHOL & ITS USES

✦ **SPIRITS AGED IN GLASS**
A large family of pure alcohol usually distilled from fermented fruit, starch and grains. Varieties include kirsch, framboise and fraises de bois. Others such as grappa, eau de vie and vodka are flavourless and are used mainly for their high alcohol content.

✦ **SPIRITS AGED IN WOOD**
Probably the most widely used alcoholic flavouring agents in the kitchen, this group includes cognac, whisky, brandy, Calvados and rum. Matured in aged wood, these robust and strong-flavoured alcohols are used in small quantities to add kick to sweet and savoury sauces.

✦ **FORTIFIED WINES**
Both sweet and dry, these are aged wines to which a spirit such as grape brandy has been added. This group, including sherries, Madeira, port, marsala and rice wine, adds sweetness and a delicate, slightly aromatic flavour.

✦ **FRUIT-FLAVOURED LIQUEURS**
A large family of blended liqueurs flavoured with various fruit juices, zests, oils and leaves. They include Grand Marnier, triple sec, Curaçao, Cointreau, cherry brandy, apricot, banana and pineapple liqueurs, and many more. They are used to impart sweetness and a good fruity aroma.

✦ **ALCOHOL FLAVOURED WITH AROMATICS**
Alcohol that has had spices and aromatics such as coffee, vanilla, cloves, bitters, herbs, zests or wood chips added to it and is then either filtered or distilled to capture the flavour — Pernod, arak and ouzo, for example. Although mainly drunk as apéritifs and digestifs, they can also be used to flavour a variety of sauces.

ALCOHOLIC SAUCES

WINES AND FORTIFIED WINES SUCH AS SHERRY, RICE WINE AND MADEIRA GIVE BODY AND FLAVOUR TO MANY SAUCES. WHITE AND RED WINES ARE USUALLY ADDED NEAR THE BEGINNING OF COOKING AND SHOULD BE REDUCED WELL BY BOILING — AS THE ALCOHOL EVAPORATES, THE FLAVOURS CONCENTRATE AND MELLOW. FORTIFIED WINES ARE GENERALLY ADDED IN SMALL QUANTITIES TOWARDS THE END OF COOKING FOR A SMOOTH, ELEGANT FINISH. SPIRITS AND LIQUEURS ARE EXTREMELY ADAPTABLE, GIVING A POWERFUL FLAVOUR BOOST TO BOTH SWEET AND SAVOURY SAUCES. FRUIT-FLAVOURED LIQUEURS CAN BE MATCHED WITH THE FLAVOUR OF YOUR SAUCE — COINTREAU IS DELICIOUS IN AN ORANGE SAUCE, FOR EXAMPLE. DON'T BE TEMPTED TO COOK WITH CHEAP WINES AND LIQUEURS: THEY PRODUCE COARSE, THIN-TASTING RESULTS.

ZABAGLIONE

MAIN IMAGE: a classic Italian dessert, zabaglione is creamy, frothy and spiked with sweet marsala wine. (*See page 128*)

COOKED VINAIGRETTE

TOP: a light orange and chicory salad drizzled with a fragrant vinaigrette laced with white wine. (*See page 69*)

RUM & GINGER BUTTER

MIDDLE: butter, rum and stem ginger being beaten together until light and creamy. (*See page 133*)

JUNIPER DEMI-GLACE

BOTTOM: red wine and gin give a robust flavour to this demi-glace served with medallions of pork and kale. (*See page 61*)

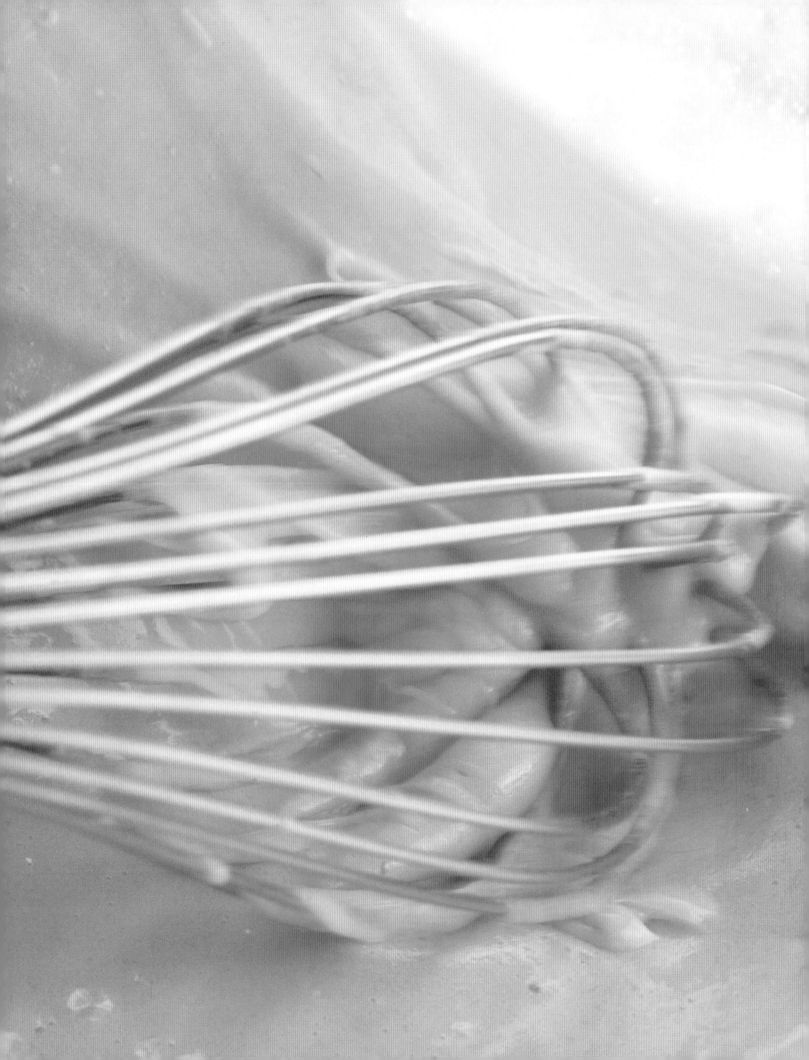

TECHNIQUES

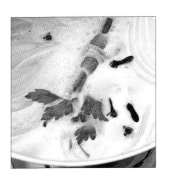

MAKING SAUCES IS NOT DIFFICULT — THEY

DO NOT REQUIRE COMPLICATED SKILLS

OR SPECIALIZED EQUIPMENT. TAKE TIME TO

MASTER A FEW SIMPLE TECHNIQUES; NOT

ONLY WILL THEY ENSURE ROBUSTLY

FLAVOURED STOCKS, FROTHY SABAYONS

AND GLOSSY MAYONNAISES, BUT THEY

WILL PROVIDE THE FOUNDATIONS ON WHICH

TO EXPERIMENT AND DEVELOP SAUCES

OF YOUR OWN.

EQUIPMENT

YOU DO NOT NEED SPECIALIZED EQUIPMENT to make a successful sauce. Most of what is shown here can be found in any reasonably well-stocked kitchen. When buying new kitchen equipment always buy the best as it will last longer. Choose equipment that feels comfortable in your hand and that is made from a non-corrosive material such as stainless steel, plastic or glass which will not react with more acidic foods.

Flat whisks: enable you to reach the corners of a pan.

Balloon whisks: suitable for whisking in bowls.

Flat-coiled wire whisks: convenient for use in bowls and pans.

BOWL PLACED OVER SAUCEPAN
An easy-to-assemble substitute for a double boiler, this provides a gentle way of cooking and heating sauces, especially hollandaise, sabayon and custard. Make sure the base of the bowl does not touch the simmering water in the pan.

PANS
Always choose heavy-bottomed pans as they conduct heat more evenly, enabling better temperature control.

WHISKS
Good for mixing and combining liquid ingredients and introducing air into a sauce, making it lighter in consistency. Select a whisk that feels comfortable and is the right weight and shape for your hand. Always buy non-corrosive stainless steel whisks.

PESTLE AND MORTAR
A traditional instrument for pounding ingredients into pastes and purées – a method that retains the full flavour and gives a texture that cannot be matched by food processors.

ELECTRICAL EQUIPMENT

Electric mixer: makes easy work of whisking mayonnaise and beating eggs, cream and butters – especially when making large quantities. For smaller quantities, use a hand-held whisk.

Mixing wand: convenient for puréeing in pans or for puréeing small quantities.

BLENDER

ELECTRIC MIXER

ELECTRIC MIXING WAND

SPICE MILL

FOOD PROCESSOR

Blender: ideal for puréeing to a smooth, fine consistency.

Food processor: good for mixing, coarse chopping and puréeing; its obvious advantage is its speed, though some argue that this can compromise flavour.

Spice mill: used for pulverizing and grinding spices. Commercially produced spice powders are finer but spices freshly ground in a spice mill are always more flavoursome.

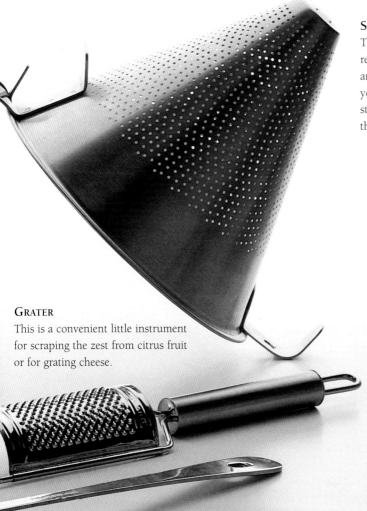

GRATER

This is a convenient little instrument for scraping the zest from citrus fruit or for grating cheese.

SIEVES

These are often essential for achieving a smooth consistency and for rescuing lumpy sauces. Both conical and round sieves are available, and all vary in fineness of mesh. Have at least two sizes of sieve in your kitchen: a larger one for straining stocks and a smaller one for straining sauces or puréeing. Clean them under running water then shake or tap to free water trapped in the mesh.

SKIMMERS

Useful for removing scum that collects on the surface of stocks and simmering sauces; always keep a bowl of cold water nearby to rinse the skimmer between skims.

LEMON SQUEEZER

Designed to fit the shape of a halved lemon, it can also be used for juicing oranges; strains the pips from the juice.

CHICKEN STOCK

NO STOCK CUBE COULD EVER COMPARE with a homemade stock prepared from fresh ingredients. As it is the basis of so many dishes, it is worthwhile preparing it yourself. You can also be creative and flavour your stock according to the dish it is intended for. The perfect chicken stock is light in colour and clear, and is achieved by using mature 'boiler' chickens, preferably free-range and organic. Bones from young roasting chickens will not do – they do not contain enough flavour and gelatine to give the stock substance. Stock freezes successfully but some flavour and texture is lost with long freezing.

MASTER RECIPE

I PREFER A ROBUST STOCK but for a more delicate flavour, reduce the quantity of vegetables. Experiment by varying them: try pumpkin, courgettes, tomatoes and even a small quantity of beetroot, as well as other herbs and spices. For an Oriental stock, include a few whole garlic cloves and make the bouquet garni with 2 halved stalks of lemongrass, a 2.5cm (1 inch) piece of ginger, sliced into strips, and 1–2 strips of orange zest. Substitute 4 star anise and ½ teaspoon of Szechwan pepper for the cloves and black peppercorns.

Makes 1–1.25 litres (1¾–2 pints)

1.5–2kg (3–4lb) chicken bones, or a whole mature chicken, cut into pieces

2 litres (3½ pints) water

1 leek, sliced

1 onion, unpeeled, washed well and cut into quarters

4 carrots, chopped

2 celery sticks, chopped

100g (3½oz) mushrooms, or 1 tsp dried wild mushrooms such as porcini (optional)

a bouquet garni made with 3 sprigs of thyme, a few celery leaves, 1 bay leaf and 2–3 strips of lemon zest (see page 30)

4 cloves and 1 tsp black peppercorns tied in a square of muslin (optional)

Shelf-life: 1 week in the refrigerator; 3 months in the freezer

1 Wash the bones or chicken pieces thoroughly in a few changes of water and drain well. Place in a large pan or a stock pot with the water and bring slowly to the boil. Skim off any residue that collects on the surface.

2 Simmer for about 30 minutes, skimming when necessary. Add the vegetables, the bouquet garni and the spice bag.

3 Continue simmering over a very low heat, uncovered, for about 1½–2 hours or until the stock has reduced by about a quarter.

4 Allow to cool a little, then strain through a muslin-lined colander. Cool as quickly as possible, then chill to remove the fat (see above).

BROWN STOCK

MADE WITH CARE and the freshest ingredients, a good brown stock is crystal clear, deep amber in colour, has no fat and is a robustly flavoured balance of vegetables and meat. Experimenting with different vegetables and herbs will subtly alter the flavour of the stock. It is the most time-consuming of the stocks and takes over three hours to prepare, which is why it is less common in domestic kitchens these days, although it is still made in good restaurants and is an essential ingredient in demi-glaces (see page 60). Traditionally made only from veal bones, it is now also made from beef, lamb or mutton bones.

(see page 60)

TROUBLESHOOTING

Clarifying a cloudy stock
Beat 1–2 egg whites with their shells and add to the stock. Bring to the boil, beating well. Boil for 3 minutes, remove from the heat and leave for 10 minutes. Skim off the crust and strain the stock through muslin.

MASTER RECIPE

ROASTING THE BONES for this stock beforehand imparts a mellow yet full and concentrated flavour and gives a rich, deep colour. Because the flavours intensify as the stock reduces, it should only be seasoned at the very end of the cooking process.

Makes 1–1.25 litres (1¾–2 pints)

1.5kg (3lb) beef, lamb or mutton bones (marrow and ribs), chopped and washed well in a few changes of water

1 calf's foot, halved and cut into quarters (optional)

3 tbsp groundnut or light olive oil

250ml (8fl oz) dry white wine

3 litres (5 pints) water

250g (8oz) carrots, chopped

2 medium onions, unpeeled, washed well and cut into quarters

2 celery sticks, chopped

2 garlic cloves, peeled

150g (5oz) mushrooms, sliced

4 very ripe tomatoes, quartered

a bouquet garni made with 4 sprigs of thyme, 2 celery leaves and 2 sprigs of parsley (see page 30)

salt and freshly ground black pepper

Shelf-life: 1 week in the refrigerator; 3 months in the freezer

1 Place the bones and the calf's foot, if using, in a roasting pan and drizzle with the oil. Brown in an oven preheated to 220°C/425°F/Gas Mark 7 for 45–50 minutes, turning the bones from time to time. Transfer the bones to a large pan.

2 Pour off the fat from the roasting pan. Over a low heat, add the wine, stirring and scraping the bottom of the pan. Pour into the pan with the bones, add the water and bring to the boil. Reduce the heat and simmer for 10 minutes.

3 Skim any residue from the surface, then add all the remaining ingredients except the salt and pepper. Simmer, uncovered, for about 3 hours.

4 Taste and season the stock. Allow to cool a little, then strain through a muslin-lined sieve and cool as quickly as possible.

FISH STOCK (FUMET)

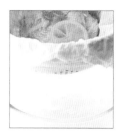

FISH STOCK, OR FUMET, IS THE BASE for many sauces and soups. Traditionally only the bones and heads of lean white fish such as sole, turbot, brill or whiting are used, but salmon, trout and bass also make a good stock. Avoid strong-flavoured oily fish such as mackerel and herring. Usually white wine is included but some recipes require red wine. For variety, try replacing the bouquet garni with aromatics such as fennel, dill, ginger, lemongrass, fennel seeds and caraway.

MASTER RECIPE

FOR A MORE INTENSELY FLAVOURED STOCK, add 1 small red mullet. For a delicate flavour, use only fish bones and no heads or trimmings. Do not simmer the stock for longer than 30 minutes as this will give it a bitter flavour.

Makes 1.25–1.5 litres (2–2½ pints)

1.5kg (3lb) fish bones, heads and trimmings

30g (1oz) unsalted butter

2 leeks, white parts only, finely sliced

1 carrot, chopped

1 celery stick, chopped

250ml (8fl oz) dry white or red wine

2.5 litres (4 pints) water

a bouquet garni made with 2 sprigs of thyme, 2 pieces of green leek leaves, 2 sprigs of parsley, 1 celery leaf and 1 bay leaf (see below)

10 peppercorns

2–3 thick slices of lemon

Shelf-life: 1 week in the refrigerator; 3 months in the freezer

BOUQUET GARNI

To make a bouquet garni, tie a bundle of fresh herbs together with string. It's an ideal way of enhancing the flavour of your stock.

1 Wash the bones thoroughly in plenty of cold water, rinsing away any traces of blood. Drain well.

2 In a pan heat the butter over a low heat and sweat the leeks, carrot and celery until soft.

3 Add the fish bones, the wine and the water and bring to the boil. Skim any sediment, then add the bouquet garni, peppercorns and lemon slices and bring back to the boil.

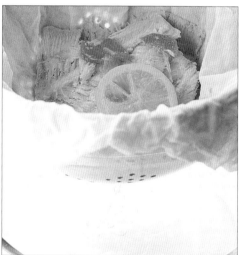

4 Reduce the heat and simmer very gently, uncovered, for 30 minutes, skimming the surface frequently. Strain through a muslin-lined colander or sieve and cool as quickly as possible.

VEGETABLE STOCK

I MAKE THIS VERY VERSATILE STOCK using a variety of vegetables and herbs, generally choosing whatever is in season. Go for flavoursome vegetables such as pumpkin, celeriac, fennel, parsley root, parsnip or mushroom, but use them sparingly so as not to overwhelm the stock with any one flavour. Include an apple, a pear or even a peach to add a little sweetness. Use this stock as a base for sauces, soups and stews and to make pilaffs and risottos.

MASTER RECIPE

EXPERIMENT BY SUBSTITUTING SPICES such as lemongrass, ginger and star anise for the bouquet garni, but make sure they are appropriate for the recipe in which you plan to use the stock. Adding 75g (2½oz) okra to the stock will thicken it, giving a slightly gelatinous texture. You can also add 2 tablespoons of either soaked barley, oats or ground rice to thicken the stock and give a velvety smoothness.

Makes 1–1.25 litres (1¾–2 pints)

1 large onion, sliced into rings

100g (3½oz) carrots, chopped

100g (3½oz) pumpkin, chopped

2 celery sticks

1 large ripe tomato, cut into quarters

3 garlic cloves, peeled

1.5 litres (2½pints) water

a bouquet garni made with 4 sprigs of parsley, 4 sprigs of coriander, 2 sprigs of thyme and 2 strips of lemon zest (see opposite)

Shelf-life: 1 week in the refrigerator; 3 months in the freezer

1 Put the chopped onion, carrots, pumpkin and celery, the quartered tomato and the garlic in a large pot and add the water.

2 Add the bouquet garni and bring to the boil. Reduce the heat and simmer, uncovered, for 25 minutes. Skim any sediment from the surface as necessary.

3 Set the stock aside to cool a little, then strain through a fine mesh conical sieve into a bowl. Cool the stock as quickly as possible.

BÉCHAMEL SAUCE

A VERSATILE BASE FOR MANY OTHER SAUCES, béchamel is used to add moisture, to bind and to enrich. It is made with a roux, which is a smooth, cooked mixture of flour and butter that binds and thickens and is also used in veloutés and some brown sauces. It is important to cook béchamel for 15 minutes so that the flour loses its raw taste and to whisk continuously to ensure a smooth and glossy consistency. Traditionally béchamel sauce is flavoured with white pepper but if, like me, you find black pepper flecks an interesting feature, use it instead as it is much more aromatic. For use as a binding agent or as a base for baked dishes, make a plain milk béchamel, but for more delicate pouring sauces use infused milk to bring out the full flavour.

TROUBLESHOOTING

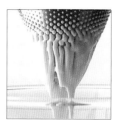

Correcting lumpy béchamel
If you have cooked the sauce too quickly or not whisked it enough, it may go lumpy. Lumps can also form if you don't stir the sauce enough and it sticks to the bottom of the pan. Either pass it through a fine sieve or process in a blender or food processor. Return to a clean pan and continue cooking.

MASTER RECIPE

BÉCHAMEL IS MADE with a white roux, which is cooked for about 4 minutes. To make a blond roux for use in veloutés, cook the roux in Step 1 for 5–6 minutes, stirring or whisking continuously, until it is a golden brown. To make a brown roux, which is sometimes used to thicken brown sauces, use clarified butter (see page 35) and cook over a medium heat, stirring or whisking continuously, for about 8–10 minutes, until it is a rich brown colour.

Makes 300ml (10fl oz)

For the roux

30g (1oz) butter

30g (1oz) plain flour

For the sauce

500ml (17fl oz) milk or
infused milk (see opposite)

freshly grated nutmeg to taste (optional)

salt and freshly ground white or black pepper

Shelf-life: 1 week in the refrigerator

1 Melt the butter in a small pan and when it starts to foam, stir in the flour with a whisk or a wooden spoon until well combined. Cook the roux over a medium heat for 3–4 minutes, stirring continuously; do not allow it to colour.

2 *Add the milk, whisking continuously to
prevent lumps forming. Bring to the boil,
then reduce the heat to minimum and simmer,
still whisking occasionally, until the sauce is
smooth, about 15–20 minutes.*

3 *Whisk in the nutmeg, if using, and season
with salt and pepper to taste.*

HOLLANDAISE

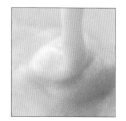

THIS LIGHT, RICH SAUCE is one of the most glorious inventions of the French kitchen although it may in fact have been created by French exiles to Holland, hence the name. It is the classic butter emulsion and resembles a warm mayonnaise but is made with clarified butter instead of oil. It is great served with boiled or steamed vegetables or fish. It is also the basis for Béarnaise Sauce (see page 54), which classically accompanies steak. After mastering the technique, you could experiment, adding different herbs, purées and spices to create new and exciting versions of this magnificent sauce. Hollandaise should be served warm, never hot. Keep it warm in a bain marie or in a bowl set over a pan of hot water (but keep the water just warmer than hand-hot and do not allow the base of the bowl to come into contact with it).

TROUBLESHOOTING

Correcting separated hollandaise
If you cook the egg yolks and the reduction too quickly or over too high a heat, or if you add the butter too fast, the sauce may separate. Start again, but use the separated sauce in place of more butter. Over a low heat, whisk 1 egg yolk with a tablespoon of water until light. Remove from the heat and gradually whisk in the separated mixture. It cannot be rescued if the eggs have coagulated.

MASTER RECIPE

THIS RICH AND SUBTLE SAUCE goes well with poached fish or steamed vegetables and is a base for many other sauces. Leftover cold hollandaise makes a surprisingly good sandwich spread.

For a slightly richer Mousseline Sauce, fold in 60ml (2fl oz) whipping cream, whipped into soft peaks, just before serving. For a deliciously nutty version of hollandaise, make noisette butter by gently heating 60g (2oz) unsalted butter until it turns a light, nutty brown and stirring it into the hollandaise just before serving.

Makes 750ml (1¼ pints)

4 tbsp water

1 tbsp white wine vinegar

1 tsp white or black peppercorns, crushed

4 egg yolks

250g (8oz) unsalted butter, clarified (see opposite), cooled to room temperature

1 tbsp lemon juice

salt

1 Put the water, vinegar and peppercorns in a small pan and simmer over a low heat until reduced by a third, about 2–3 minutes. Strain the reduction through a sieve into a glass or stainless steel bowl, then set aside to cool.

2 Place the bowl over a pan of just-simmering water, add the egg yolks and whisk until the mixture has thickened and is smooth, about 5–8 minutes. Keep the heat low and do not allow the sauce to get hotter than hand-hot, or the eggs might coagulate (see above).

CLARIFYING BUTTER

Melt the butter in a small pan over a very low heat, then let it froth for a few seconds. Skim the froth from the surface, then set the butter aside to cool slightly. Strain the cooled butter through a muslin-lined sieve, leaving the milky sediment behind in the bottom of the pan. Rinsing the muslin in cold water before use and then wringing it out helps to catch any remaining froth.

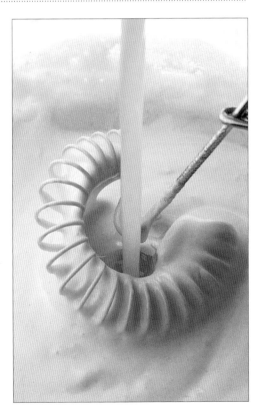

3 *Slowly pour in the cooled, clarified butter, whisking continuously until the sauce is thick and fluffy. Mix in the lemon juice and the salt.*

4 *Smooth, thick and creamy, the hollandaise should now hold the trail of the whisk. Serve immediately.*

SABAYON

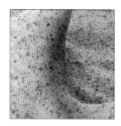

A CLOSE RELATIVE OF ITALIAN ZABAGLIONE (see page 128), sabayon is usually a sweet sauce. However, instead of the classic sweet wine and sugar, this savoury rendition uses stock, vermouth and herbs beaten together with egg yolks over a gentle heat to produce a light and airy sauce.

The resulting sabayon is frothy in texture and surprisingly low in fat. As with other sauces containing egg, sabayon should be heated gently and never allowed to approach boiling, or the eggs might coagulate. Sabayon is a marvellous sauce – it never fails to impress yet once you have mastered it you will find that it is quick and not at all difficult to prepare. Sabayon should be served immediately, while it is still warm. See pages 56–57 for further recipes.

TROUBLESHOOTING

What can go wrong

Sabayon is quick and easy to make but if you whisk it for too long you risk overworking it, which will result in a dense and heavy texture. If you cook it over too high a heat, or allow the base of the bowl to come into contact with the simmering water in the pan, it may separate and the eggs may coagulate. Unfortunately, little can be done to retrieve it; start again.

MASTER RECIPE

THIS IS A DELICATE, HERB-FLECKED SABAYON, delicious with shellfish and poached fish. For a sabayon to serve with grilled chicken or other poultry, replace the fish stock with 150ml (1/4 pint) chicken stock that has been boiled and reduced down to about 60ml (2fl oz). Substitute 45ml (1 1/2 fl oz) white wine for the vermouth and orange juice for the lemon juice.

Serves 4–6

4 egg yolks

1 tsp sugar

45ml (1 1/2 fl oz) Fish Stock (see page 30)

30ml (1fl oz) dry vermouth

3 tbsp Herb Purée (see page 42)

1 tbsp lemon juice

salt and freshly ground black pepper

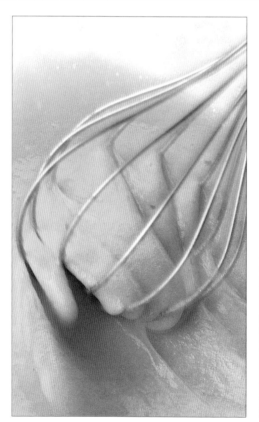

1 Place the egg yolks in a large bowl, add the sugar and beat, either by hand or with an electric whisk, until the mixture is well combined and has turned slightly paler.

2 Add the fish stock, the dry vermouth and the herb purée and continue to beat until they are all mixed in.

3 Place the bowl over a pan of just-simmering water, making sure the water does not touch the base of the bowl. Whisk until the sauce is thick and frothy, about 8–10 minutes. If you are using an electric whisk, this will only take about 5 minutes.

4 The sabayon is ready when it is thick enough to leave a ribbon trail on the surface when the whisk is lifted from the bowl. Finish by whisking in the lemon juice, then season to taste and serve immediately.

MAYONNAISE

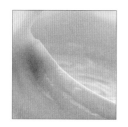

MAKING MAYONNAISE IS A MAGICAL PROCESS: egg yolks, oil and seasoning are transformed into a rich, glossy emulsion that can be flavoured in a multitude of ways. A favourite of the cold table, mayonnaise can be used to dress salads, as a dip, as an accompaniment to cold meats or seafood, or to transform sandwiches and canapés. The secret of success is to make sure all the ingredients are at cool room temperature before you begin. The optional boiling water added at the end extends the storage life of the mayonnnaise and acts as a binding agent, correcting the consistency if necessary. Making mayonnaise by hand requires plenty of elbow grease, but you can achieve nearly as impressive results in a fraction of the time using an electric whisk or food processor (see opposite).

TROUBLESHOOTING

Correcting curdled mayonnaise
Place 2 tablespoons of the curdled mayonnaise in a clean bowl and add either 2 teaspoons of made-up mustard or an egg yolk and whisk until well amalgamated. Whisk in the rest of the curdled mayonnaise a little at a time, until thick and glossy. Whisk in the boiling water, if using, and the extra lemon juice or vinegar and seasoning.

MASTER RECIPE

FOR A STRONGER OLIVE OIL FLAVOUR, substitute extra-virgin olive oil for one third of the oil. For a nutty-flavoured mayonnaise, replace half the oil with either hazelnut or walnut oil.

Makes 300ml (10fl oz)

2 egg yolks, at cool room temperature

2 tsp lemon juice or white wine vinegar, plus a little extra to taste

1 tsp Dijon mustard or mustard powder

a small pinch of salt

300ml (10fl oz) groundnut or light olive oil

2 tbsp boiling water (optional)

salt and freshly ground pepper

Shelf-life: 1 week in the refrigerator

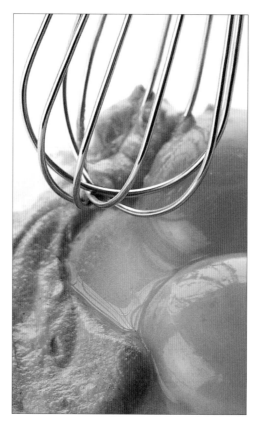

1 Place a mat or tea towel under a mixing bowl to prevent it from slipping. Put the egg yolks, lemon juice or vinegar, mustard and salt in the bowl and whisk together with a balloon whisk until well amalgamated.

2 Start adding the oil one drop at a time, whisking continuously, until about one third of it has been incorporated and the mayonnaise is beginning to thicken. It is important not to add the oil too quickly at this stage, or the mayonnaise will curdle (see above).

MACHINE METHODS

Using an Electric Whisk

Whisk the egg yolks, lemon juice or vinegar, mustard and salt on high speed for a few seconds. Reduce the speed to medium and add the oil a little at a time until one third has been incorporated. Add the rest of the oil in a thin, steady stream until the mayonnaise is thick and glossy, then increase the speed to maximum and finish as in step 3.

Using a Food Processor or Blender

Process the egg yolks, lemon juice or vinegar, mustard and salt for a few seconds. With the machine running, add the oil in a thin, steady stream until the mayonnaise is thick and glossy. Finish as in step 3, but process for only 1–2 seconds to incorporate the extra ingredients.

4 Cream-coloured and glossy, the mayonnaise is rich and thick in consistency and forms stiff peaks.

3 Pour in the rest of the oil in a thin, steady stream, whisking constantly, until the mayonnaise is thick and glossy and forms stiff peaks. Whisk in the extra lemon juice or vinegar and seasoning to taste. If the mayonnaise is to be kept, whisk in the boiling water.

CRÈME ANGLAISE

THE ULTIMATE DESSERT SAUCE, crème anglaise, or custard, can be served hot or chilled and has numerous uses. Delicious poured over fruit and hot and cold puddings, it is also an essential ingredient for trifle. Set with gelatine, it makes a base for bavarois, while mixed with fruit or other flavourings then frozen, it is transformed into ice-cream. Try flavouring custard with anything from cinnamon sticks and bitter almonds to orange zest, lavender, spirits and liqueurs. See page 126 for further recipes.

See page 126 for further recipes.

TROUBLESHOOTING

Correcting curdled custard
If the custard has been overcooked or allowed to boil, it will curdle. Pass it through a sieve or process in a blender, then return to a clean pan. Add 2 teaspoons of arrowroot or cornflour slaked with 2 tablespoons of milk (see page 44). Cook over gentle heat, whisking constantly and not allowing it to boil, for 1–2 minutes or until thick enough to coat the back of a spoon.

MASTER RECIPE

CUSTARD CAN BE MADE directly on the heat but this requires practice as it should never be allowed to get hotter than 80°C/175°F. A bowl set over a pan of just-simmering water or a double boiler are surer ways of controlling heat level and preventing the custard curdling. To cool custard, pour into a clean bowl set in a bowl of ice. Whisk from time to time to prevent a skin forming. Lay clingfilm directly on the surface and refrigerate.

Makes 300ml (10fl oz)

1 vanilla pod, sliced in half lengthways, or 1 tsp natural vanilla extract

500ml (17fl oz) milk

6 egg yolks

3–4 tbsp caster sugar, or to taste

Shelf-life: 1 week in the refrigerator

PREPARING A VANILLA POD

Slice the pod in half lengthways and, holding one end of the pod, run a sharp knife down the length of it. The seeds will scrape off.

1 Scrape the vanilla pod (see left) and add the seeds and pod or the extract to the milk in a pan. Whisking, bring slowly to the boil, then reduce the heat and simmer for 5 minutes.

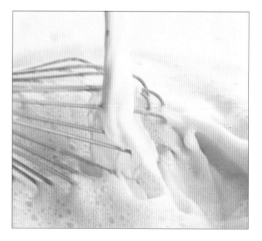

2 In a bowl, beat the egg yolks and sugar until the mixture has lightened and become foamy. Pour the boiling milk on to the egg mixture, whisking continuously.

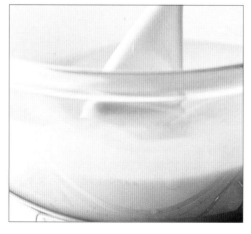

3 Place the bowl over a pan of just-simmering water, making sure the base does not touch the water, or transfer the mixture, together with the vanilla pod, to the top of a double boiler.

4 Stir continuously until the sauce is thick enough to coat the back of a spoon, about 10–15 minutes. Do not allow the custard to boil. Remove the vanilla pod, if using, and stir well.

CARAMEL

GOLDEN AND CRYSTAL CLEAR, caramel is simply sugar syrup (see page 128) that has been boiled until all the water has evaporated. When it reaches 154°C/309°F it starts to caramelize and gives off a pleasant aroma. Use hot caramel to line moulds for *crème caramel* or to make spun sugar by pouring it on a lightly greased ladle to set. Set and then broken up, caramel makes a good crunchy topping and can also be used in powder form to add instant flavour to sweet sauces and custards (see right).

(see page 128)

CARAMEL CRUNCH

To make caramel crunch, or powder, crush the broken shards in a pestle and mortar until fine.

MASTER RECIPE

THE LAST STAGES in the cooking process are crucial and happen very quickly, so be on guard and watch constantly. In no time at all caramel can start smoking and then burn – at which point it is irretrievable. To stop the caramel cooking further, plunge the base of the pan into cold water the instant the right colour is achieved.

Makes 300ml (10fl oz) liquid caramel or 250g (8oz) caramel crunch

250g (8oz) caster sugar

5 tbsp water

Shelf-life: up to 1 year as shards or a crushed powder, stored in a tightly sealed jar

1 Place the sugar and water in a pan and heat gently, shaking the pan occasionally, until all the sugar has dissolved. Bring slowly to the boil and the syrup will begin to caramelize.

2 It should turn from pale gold to light brown, then to dark brown. Remove from the heat and plunge the base of the pan into cold water as soon as the right colour is achieved.

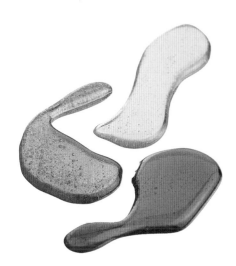

3 When the caramel reaches the desired colour and consistency, it is ready for use in its liquid form or it can be carefully poured on to a lightly oiled surface to set.

4 Leave the caramel to cool and set, then crack it with a pestle, wooden mallet or rolling pin. The caramel shards make an elegant cake decoration.

HERB PURÉE

THIS IS AN EASY WAY OF ADDING INSTANT COLOUR and flavour to sauces and dips. Fresh herbs are blanched briefly then puréed, which captures their flavour and extends their storage life. The purée can be refrigerated or frozen (use ice-cube trays, see pages 134–35). Tender, mild herbs such as flat-leaf parsley, basil, dill, spinach and sorrel – or a mixture of them all – work best. Strong-flavoured herbs with tough leaves, such as thyme, sage and rosemary, tend to be bitter and difficult to purée.

MASTER RECIPE

THIS IS THE QUICKEST and most convenient way that I know of storing fresh herbs. Remember to blanch the herbs only briefly, otherwise their flavours will be destroyed. To achieve a smooth purée, spend time removing any tough stems or leaves; use young, bright green leaves and discard any that are wilted or discoloured.

Makes 100g (3½oz)

1 litre (1¾ pints) water

2 tsp caster sugar

150g (5oz) fresh herbs, leaves only

a little olive oil

Shelf-life: 1 week in the refrigerator; 3 months in the freezer

1 Bring the water to a rapid boil and stir in the sugar. Add the herbs and bring back to the boil, then immediately remove from the heat and fish out the herbs with a skimmer or slotted spoon.

2 Plunge the blanched leaves into a large bowl of iced water. Swirl the wilted leaves around, then drain. Squeeze out all the remaining water with your hands.

3 Put the blanched herbs into a food processor with 1–2 tablespoons of water and process into a fine purée, or chop very finely by hand using a mezzaluna.

4 Rinse a large piece of muslin in cold water, wring well, then use, doubled, to line a sieve. Place over a deep bowl, pour in the herb purée and leave to drain in a cool place for 2 hours.

5 Pour away any liquid that has collected in the bowl and scrape the purée into a small dish. Pour a thin layer of olive oil over the purée, cover and refrigerate.

TOMATO PURÉE

THIS FRESH TOMATO PURÉE is far superior to shop-bought tomato purée. I use it to add a delicate pink tint and a remarkably fragrant tomato flavour to many dishes; it is also very useful for thickening sauces, soups and stews. It is important to use ripe, firm-fleshed tomatoes, such as Italian plum or beef tomatoes, and, where possible, to choose vine-ripened ones as they are brightly coloured and usually sweeter in flavour.

MASTER RECIPE

I MAKE THIS IN LARGE QUANTITIES whenever ripe, fragrant tomatoes are available. You needn't pour away the surprisingly clear juice that drains from the tomatoes – it is very flavoursome and makes a delicious base for soups.

Makes 100g (3½oz)

1kg (2lb) fragrant cooking tomatoes, peeled, deseeded (see below) and coarsely chopped

3 tbsp lemon juice

a little olive oil

Shelf-life: 1 week in the refrigerator; 3 months in the freezer

1 Put the tomatoes and lemon juice in a food processor and process until a smooth purée is achieved. Rinse a large piece of muslin in cold water, wring well, then use, doubled, to line a colander or sieve.

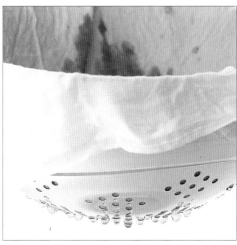

2 Place the muslin-lined colander or sieve over a deep bowl, then pour in the processed tomato. Cover with clingfilm and leave to drain in the refrigerator for about 2 hours.

PEELING TOMATOES

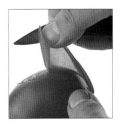

With a sharp knife, cut out the core, then make a slit down the side of each tomato. Put the tomatoes in a bowl, pour over boiling water to cover and leave to stand for a couple of minutes. The hot water loosens the skin and it can then be easily peeled away with a sharp knife.

To deseed, simply cut the tomato into quarters and scrape away the seeds.

3 Pour away the clear tomato juice that has collected in the bottom of the bowl (or reserve it for future use). Scrape the purée into a small dish.

4 Pour a thin layer of olive oil over the purée, cover and refrigerate.

THICKENING SAUCES

MODERN COOKS TEND TO SERVE LIGHTER, THINNER SAUCES and to avoid using heavy starches. Yet there are always variables when cooking and from time to time a thickener is needed to achieve the right consistency. The most common technique for thickening is through reduction – rapid boiling until a glossy, syrupy consistency is reached. Sauces can also be thickened with the addition of starch such as cornflour or arrowroot, which expands when added to a boiling liquid and absorbs the liquid to give a permanent, thickened suspension. Although each technique gives a slightly different finish to a sauce, many are interchangeable; consult Troubleshooting on pages 136–37 for specific advice.

THICKENING WITH CORNFLOUR

THIS GIVES A SHINY, light and opaque finish to almost any sauce. Usually 2–3 teaspoons of cornflour are enough for about 500ml (17fl oz) liquid; mix equal quantities of cornflour and a cool liquid such as water, stock or wine – a process known as slaking. Add the mixture to the sauce a little at a time and boil briefly until the right consistency is achieved.

1 Mix the cornflour and liquid until a smooth paste of pouring consistency is achieved.

2 Pour the mixture into boiling sauce and boil for 1 minute, whisking or stirring continuously.

3 The thickened sauce will coat the back of a spoon. The sauce will not thin if boiled or reheated.

THICKENING WITH ARROWROOT

ONE OF THE MOST VERSATILE thickeners, arrowroot produces a clear, light sauce that can also be used as a glaze. Add about 2–3 teaspoons of arrowroot for 500ml (17fl oz) liquid, although you may need to add a little more if the liquid is acidic. As with cornflour, use equal quantities of arrowroot and a cool liquid such as water, stock or wine.

1 Mix the arrowroot and liquid until a smooth, pourable paste is achieved.

2 Pour the mixture into boiling sauce and boil, whisking or stirring, for no longer than a minute.

3 The sauce thickens immediately and becomes glossy; it evenly coats the back of a spoon.

THICKENING BY REDUCTION

THIS TECHNIQUE gives an intensely flavoured, aromatic sauce that is best served in small quantities. Use this method of thickening for demi-glaces, gravies and stock-based sauces. Skimming the sauce from time to time while it reduces can prevent the sauce from becoming cloudy.

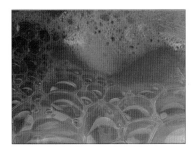

1 Boil the sauce over a medium heat; as it reduces and the water evaporates, it should thicken.

2 The sauce will continue to thicken for as long as you continue to boil it.

THICKENING WITH BUTTER

THE PROCESS OF ADDING butter to a sauce to thicken it is known as mounting (from the French *monter*); it produces a creamy, glossy sauce that thinly coats the back of a spoon. Always use fresh, well-chilled unsalted butter and be sure to add it a little at a time. Finish the sauce with a few drops of lemon juice and serve immediately.

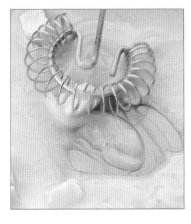

1 Bring the sauce to the boil, then, off the heat, whisk in chilled cubes of unsalted butter.

2 Add the butter gradually until the sauce is rich and glossy and coats the back of a spoon.

QUICK TIPS

Thickening with breadcrumbs
To thicken and add substance to salsas, soups and sauces such as bread sauce, sprinkle in breadcrumbs by the handful. Stir in and leave to stand until any excess liquid has been absorbed. You can also use burghul, oatmeal, crumbled crackers or rusks, or ground almonds instead of breadcrumbs.

Thickening with fruit purées
Use fresh or dried fruit purées to add texture and sweetness to coulis and sauces.

Thickening with vegetable purées
Add mashed root vegetables, such as carrots, parsnips and celeriac to sauces, soups and stews to thicken and improve the texture and consistency.

THICKENING WITH BEURRE MANIÉ (KNEADED BUTTER)

IDEAL FOR THICKENING and adding gloss to soups, stews and gravies, beurre manié is the kitchen's most valuable fixer. It should be added in small quantities until the right consistency is achieved. Use only unsalted butter to make beurre manié. It can be prepared in advance and frozen.

1 With a palette knife, mash equal quantities of plain flour and softened butter into a smooth paste.

2 Gradually add the paste to boiling sauce, stirring or whisking until it has dispersed.

3 Boil for 2–3 minutes to cook the flour. The sauce should thicken enough to coat the spoon.

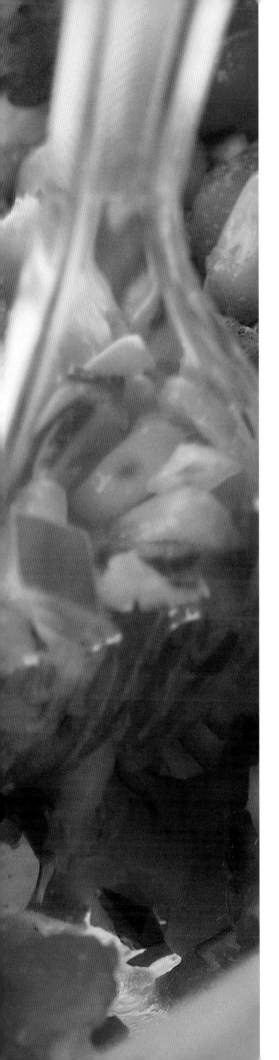

RECIPES

FROM CLASSICS SUCH AS HOLLANDAISE AND

BÉCHAMEL TO SIMPLE DRESSINGS AND

SALSAS, THE FOLLOWING PAGES CELEBRATE

SAUCES IN THE BROADEST SENSE OF THE

WORD. A MEDLEY OF RECIPES IS OFFERED;

SOME ARE OLD FAVOURITES WHILE OTHERS

HAVE BEEN SPECIALLY CREATED FOR THIS

BOOK. LOOK FOR NOVEL AND IMAGINATIVE

WAYS TO SERVE THESE VERSATILE SAUCES.

CLASSIC SAUCES

IT IS DIFFICULT TO DEFINE CLASSIC SAUCES — WHAT IS CLASSIC IN ONE COUNTRY MIGHT BE COMPLETELY

ALIEN TO ANOTHER. THE SAUCES IN THIS CHAPTER ARE MOSTLY FRENCH IN ORIGIN, BUT MANY ARE

REPRESENTATIVE OF NEW TRENDS IN MODERN CUISINE — FOR EXAMPLE, THEY MAY BE LIGHTER THAN

TRADITIONAL SAUCES OR USE EXOTIC INGREDIENTS THAT ARE NOW MORE READILY AVAILABLE.

WHITE SAUCES

BÉCHAMEL-BASED SAUCES are quick and straightforward to make as well as being incredibly versatile. A cheese version is wonderful on pasta; others can be poured over fish, eggs or vegetables and lightly grilled until golden. Béchamel-based sauces will last for up to a week in the refrigerator. They should be reheated gently; you may need to add a little milk to improve the consistency. The master recipe for Béchamel is on pages 32–33.

SOUBISE

Named after a French army commander, this smooth and satisfying sauce is especially good with lamb, roasted poultry and game birds. Traditionally this sauce is sieved, but for a more intense onion flavour, simply process in a blender or food processor until smooth.

Advance preparation: the béchamel can be made in advance

Shelf-life: 3 days in the refrigerator (brush the top with butter to prevent a skin forming); 3 months in the freezer

50g (1¾oz) butter
300g (10oz) onions, finely chopped
1 quantity of Béchamel (see pages 32–33)
3 tbsp double cream
freshly grated nutmeg to taste
strained lemon juice to taste (optional)
salt and freshly ground white or black pepper

1 Melt the butter in a small pan, add the onions, then cover and sweat until soft and translucent, about 10–15 minutes.

2 Meanwhile, in a separate pan, heat the béchamel to boiling point. Add it to the onions and slowly bring to the boil, stirring continuously. Reduce the heat as soon as it reaches boiling point and simmer, stirring frequently, for 30 minutes, or until the onions are very tender.

3 Process the sauce in a food processor or blender, or pass it through a sieve into a clean pan, pushing through as much of the onion as possible. Add the cream.

4 Bring to the boil, reduce the heat and simmer, stirring constantly, for about 5–8 minutes, until it is the consistency of porridge. Season to taste with the nutmeg, lemon juice, if using, and salt and pepper.

VARIATION

CARAMELIZED SOUBISE
Serve this modern take on Soubise with vegetables and game birds. Follow the recipe above but use only 30g (1oz) butter and add 2 tablespoons olive oil. Increase the amount of onion to 500g (1lb). When the onions are translucent, increase the heat to medium and add 1 tablespoon soft dark brown sugar and 2 tablespoons balsamic vinegar. Cook for a further 15–20 minutes until golden and caramelized, then add the hot béchamel and finish as for Soubise. For a thinner consistency, stir in 1–2 tablespoons milk or cream.

MUSHROOM SAUCE

A vegetarian version of Supreme Sauce (see page 53) that goes as well with cooked vegetables as it does with roast chicken. This sauce can be served smooth but I prefer to leave in the mushrooms.

Advance preparation: the béchamel can be made in advance

Shelf-life: 3 days in the refrigerator (brush the top with butter to prevent a skin forming); 3 months in the freezer

1 quantity of Béchamel (see pages 32–33)
100g (3½ oz) button mushrooms, thinly sliced
1 tbsp lemon juice
grated lemon zest to taste
¼ tsp sweet paprika
cayenne pepper to taste
30g (1oz) butter, chilled and cubed
salt

1 Heat the béchamel to boiling point, add the mushrooms and simmer over a very low heat for about 10 minutes. Stir the sauce continuously to prevent it catching on the bottom of the pan.

2 Remove from the heat and either leave the mushrooms in the sauce or strain the sauce through a sieve to remove them.

3 Add the lemon juice and zest and the paprika, then add cayenne pepper and salt to taste. Beat in the butter a few pieces at a time until melted, then serve.

ROBUST MUSHROOM SAUCE

50g (1¾oz) butter
100g (3½oz) brown-cap mushrooms, chopped
15g (½oz) dried porcini mushrooms, soaked in 60ml (2fl oz) hot water for 30 minutes
1 quantity of Béchamel (see pages 32–33)
1 tbsp soy sauce
1 tbsp lemon juice
¼ tsp grated lemon zest
1–2 tbsp chopped fresh chervil or parsley
salt and freshly ground black pepper

1 Heat the butter in a small pan, add the fresh mushrooms and sweat until softened, about 5 minutes. Drain the porcini, reserving the soaking liquid, chop them finely and add to the pan. Fry for about 2 minutes, then strain in the porcini soaking liquid and add the béchamel and soy sauce. Simmer the sauce for 20 minutes.

2 Remove from the heat and stir in the lemon juice and zest. Season to taste and stir in the chervil or parsley.

This is very quick to make and delicious with beef, game birds and even pasta. If you prefer a smoother consistency, purée the sauce in a blender or food processor, or strain through a sieve before seasoning.

Advance preparation: the béchamel can be made in advance

Shelf-life: 3 days in the refrigerator (brush the top with butter to prevent a skin forming); 3 months in the freezer

MORNAY SAUCE

This classic cheese sauce is traditionally flavoured with Emmenthal, Gruyère or farmhouse Cheddar, but you could experiment with freshly grated Parmesan, Spanish Manchego or, for an orange cheese sauce, red Leicester. For a lighter version, omit the cream.

Advance preparation: the béchamel can be made in advance

Shelf-life: 3 days in the refrigerator (brush the top with butter to prevent a skin forming); 3 months in the freezer

See page 19 for illustration

1 quantity of Béchamel (see pages 32–33)
75ml (2½fl oz) double cream
100g (3½oz) Emmenthal, Gruyère or farmhouse Cheddar, grated
freshly grated nutmeg to taste
freshly ground black pepper

1 Place the béchamel and cream in a small pan and heat to boiling point. Lower the heat and bubble gently, whisking continuously to prevent sticking, for about 5 minutes.

2 Add the cheese and whisk for about a minute, or until all the cheese has melted and the sauce is smooth.

3 Remove from the heat and whisk in nutmeg and pepper to taste.

VARIATION

BLUE CHEESE SAUCE

Follow the recipe for Mornay, but use only 60ml (2fl oz) double cream and stir in 75g (2½oz) freshly grated Parmesan in place of the Emmenthal, Gruyère or Cheddar. Stir in 100g (3½oz) crumbled blue cheese, such as gorgonzola with the nutmeg, plus 4–5 shredded sage leaves and seasoning to taste. Heat for about 1 minute to melt the cheese, then serve.

EXOTIC BÉCHAMEL

An interesting take on the classic béchamel, this exotic sauce is particularly good with steamed vegetables and grilled oily fish. The secret of its light texture is the long simmering time. For a smoother sauce, use stone-ground white flour. Using coconut milk, soy milk or any alternative 'milks' makes a good vegan option.

Shelf-life: 1 week in the refrigerator; 3 months in the freezer

2 tbsp groundnut or sunflower oil
40g (1½oz) wholemeal flour
500ml (17 fl oz) coconut milk or Infused Milk (see page 33)
30g (1oz) fresh ginger, finely shredded
50g (1¾oz) shallots, finely chopped
1 garlic clove, finely chopped
1 red chilli, deseeded and finely chopped
1 tbsp lime juice
salt

1 Heat the oil in a pan, add the flour and cook, stirring, until it begins to smell pleasantly nutty, about 4–5 minutes.

2 Add the milk and bring slowly to the boil, whisking continuously to prevent the sauce sticking to the bottom of the pan.

3 When the sauce has thickened to the consistency of double cream, transfer it to a double boiler or a bowl placed over a pan of simmering water. Cover and steam gently for about 45 minutes, whisking frequently to prevent a skin forming.

4 Add all the remaining ingredients except the lime juice and salt, and steam for a further 15 minutes, whisking frequently. Remove from the heat, whisk in the lime juice, add salt to taste and serve immediately.

AURORA ▷

½ quantity of Béchamel (see pages 32–33)
75ml (2½fl oz) double cream
125g (4oz) Cooked Tomato Coulis (see page 59) or Tomato Purée (see page 43)
30g (1oz) butter, chilled and cubed
1 tsp lemon juice
fresh basil leaves, shredded (optional)
cayenne pepper to taste
salt and freshly ground black pepper

1 Combine the béchamel and cream in a small pan, bring to the boil and simmer for about 5 minutes.

2 Add the tomato coulis or purée and simmer for 5 minutes, whisking constantly.

3 Remove from the heat and whisk in the butter a little at a time. Pass the sauce through a sieve, add the lemon juice, basil, if using, and cayenne and season to taste.

A tomato-flavoured béchamel that is best served with turkey, chicken or vegetables. If you prefer, use bought tomato purée, but add 1–2 tablespoons of grated onion, 1 grated garlic clove and a sprig of sage, thyme or rosemary to boost the flavour.

Advance preparation: the béchamel can be made in advance

Shelf-life: 3 days in the refrigerator

PARSLEY SAUCE

1 quantity of Béchamel (see pages 32–33)
60ml (2 fl oz) double cream (optional)
3 tbsp chopped fresh parsley
1 tsp lemon juice
finely grated lemon zest to taste
salt and freshly ground black pepper

1 Bring the béchamel and cream to the boil in a pan, then remove from the heat.

2 Stir in the parsley, lemon juice and zest. Season to taste and serve.

Traditionally served with cooked ham, parsley sauce is also good with grilled or steamed fish or chicken.

Advance preparation: the béchamel can be made in advance

Shelf-life: 3 days in the refrigerator

VARIATION

MIXED HERB SAUCE
To make a herb sauce, delicious with steamed vegetables or poached chicken, follow the recipe above but beat in 2–3 tablespoons hazelnut oil instead of the cream. Remove from the heat and stir in a tablespoon each of chopped fresh tarragon, thyme and chervil in place of the parsley.

OPPOSITE: AURORA REACHES THE PERFECT CONSISTENCY

VELOUTÉ SAUCES

RICH AND VELVETY, VELOUTÉ SAUCE is made from the same roux base as Béchamel (see pages 32–33) but using stock instead of milk makes it thinner and lighter. The flavour depends on the quality of your stock: homemade is best but commercially produced fresh stock will do – stock cubes should only be used in emergencies. Use a stock that complements the food you are serving: chicken stock with chicken, for example.

VELOUTÉ

The ideal consistency of a velouté is that of a smooth pouring sauce that thinly coats the back of a spoon. If a thicker consistency is preferred, stir in up to 50g (1³/₄oz) beurre manié (see page 45) before straining and simmer for a further 5–8 minutes.

Advance preparation: the stock can be made in advance

Shelf-life: 2–3 days in the refrigerator; 1 month in the freezer

1 quantity of White or Blonde Roux (see page 32)
750ml (1¼ pints) Stock (see pages 28–31)
strained lemon juice to taste (optional)
salt and freshly ground black pepper

1 Heat the roux in a small pan, then add the stock and bring to the boil, whisking continuously with a wire whisk.

2 Reduce the heat to minimum and simmer the velouté for 30 minutes, skimming any residue off the surface and whisking every now and then.

3 Pass the velouté through a sieve, add lemon juice, if liked, and season to taste.

CAPER SAUCE

This delicious British sauce is traditionally served with boiled mutton but is also surprisingly good with chicken and fish.

Advance preparation: the velouté can be made in advance

Shelf-life: 2–3 days in the refrigerator

1 quantity of Velouté made with Chicken, Mutton or Lamb Stock (see above)
3 tbsp capers in brine, drained and chopped
1–2 anchovy fillets, chopped (optional)
1 tbsp lemon juice
a few gratings of lemon zest
2 tbsp chopped fresh parsley, mint or dill
salt and freshly ground black pepper

1 Bring the velouté to the boil in a pan and add the capers and the anchovies, if using. Reduce the heat and simmer for 10 minutes, stirring frequently to prevent scorching.

2 Season, then add the lemon juice and zest. Stir in the herbs just before serving.

LEMONGRASS & COCONUT SAUCE

50g (1³/₄oz) butter
100g (3½oz) shallots, finely chopped
2 lemongrass stalks, hard outer layers removed, finely chopped
1 garlic clove, finely chopped
2 tbsp plain flour, sifted
250ml (8fl oz) Fish Stock (see page 30)
250ml (8fl oz) coconut milk
1 small red chilli, chopped
4 kaffir lime leaves, finely shredded
1 tsp palm sugar or light soft brown sugar (optional)
2 tbsp lime juice
2 tbsp Thai fish sauce (*nam pla*) or salt

A spicy, piquant sauce, best served with grilled or fried firm-fleshed Pacific fish such as barramundi or kingclip. It also goes well with white fish such as cod or halibut.

Advance preparation: the stock can be made in advance

Shelf-life: 2–3 days in the refrigerator

1 Heat the butter in a small pan, add the shallots, lemongrass and garlic and fry gently, stirring often, until the shallots start to colour, about 5 minutes. Sprinkle in the flour and cook, stirring, until the shallots are lightly browned, about 4–5 minutes.

2 Add the fish stock and coconut milk, whisking well to incorporate any bits that have stuck to the bottom of the pan. Bring to the boil, then reduce the heat and bubble gently for about 30 minutes, whisking from time to time to prevent sticking.

3 Pass the sauce through a sieve into a clean pan. Add the chilli, kaffir lime leaves and sugar, if using. Bring to the boil, then reduce the heat and simmer for 2 minutes. Remove from the heat and stir in the lime juice and fish sauce or salt.

SUPREME SAUCE

A classic sauce for chicken, and one of the most delicate. If you prefer more texture, do not sieve the sauce.

Advance preparation: the velouté can be made in advance

Shelf-life: 2–3 days in the refrigerator

1 quantity of Velouté made with Chicken Stock (see opposite)
75g (2½oz) button mushrooms or mushroom stalks, thinly sliced
4 tbsp double cream
30g (1oz) butter, chilled and cubed
lemon juice to taste (optional)
4 tbsp dry sherry (optional)
salt and freshly ground black pepper

1 Heat the velouté in a small pan. Stir in the mushrooms and cream and simmer gently for about 10 minutes, stirring frequently to prevent sticking.

2 Pass the sauce through a sieve into a clean pan. Over a medium heat, beat in the butter, one piece at a time. Remove from the heat, add the lemon juice and sherry, if using, season to taste and serve.

OLIVE OIL SAUCE

A robust and tasty sauce that is very low in cholesterol since the roux is made with olive oil instead of butter. It marries well with chicken or grilled fish. You could use tinned roasted and peeled peppers instead.

Advance preparation: the stock can be made in advance

Shelf-life: 2–3 days in the refrigerator

60g (2oz) plain flour
4 tbsp extra-virgin olive oil
500ml (17 fl oz) Chicken Stock (see page 28)
1 large red pepper, roasted, peeled, deseeded and finely chopped (see page 96)
75g (2½oz) green olives, stoned and chopped
1 garlic clove, crushed to a paste with a little salt
2 tbsp chopped fresh flat-leaf parsley (optional)
salt and freshly ground black pepper

1 Make a roux with the flour and 3 tablespoons of the oil (see page 32). Add the stock and bring to the boil, stirring.

2 Reduce the heat and skim any scum from the surface. Add the red pepper and simmer for 30 minutes, stirring frequently.

3 Add the olives and garlic and simmer for 2–3 minutes. Season, beat in the rest of the oil and stir in the parsley, if using.

MUSTARD SAUCE

75ml (2½fl oz) white wine
75ml (2½fl oz) orange juice
½ tsp grated orange zest
1 tbsp white wine vinegar
½ tsp coriander seeds, crushed
2 tsp English mustard powder
1 quantity of Velouté made with Chicken Stock (see left)
3 tbsp double cream or crème fraîche
2 tbsp wholegrain mustard
salt and freshly ground black pepper

This light orange- and mustard-flavoured sauce is delicious with roast or poached poultry.

Advance preparation: the velouté can be made in advance

Shelf-life: 2–3 days in the refrigerator

1 Place the wine, orange juice and zest, vinegar, coriander seeds and mustard powder in a small pan and bring to a rapid boil, whisking well. Boil for 8–10 minutes, until the liquid has reduced to 3 tablespoons. Remove from the heat and strain the reduction into a clean pan.

2 Heat the velouté, then stir it into the strained reduction and bring to the boil. Reduce the heat and simmer for 5 minutes, whisking frequently. Whisk in the cream and mustard, then season to taste and serve.

VARIATION

MUSTARD SAUCE FOR FISH

Easily adapted, this sauce makes a delectable accompaniment to poached fish, salmon in particular. Substitute fish stock (see page 30) for the chicken stock and fennel seeds for the coriander seeds.

BUTTER EMULSIONS

THESE SAUCES ARE A DELICATE MIXTURE of butter and egg yolks, emulsified by vigorous whisking over a gentle heat. The finished sauce should be thick, opaque and creamy. The classic butter emulsion is Hollandaise, invented by French Huguenots exiled in Holland. The master recipe for this can be found on pages 34–35.

BÉARNAISE SAUCE

A more robust version of Hollandaise (see pages 34–35), this sauce is best suited to grilled meats and salmon.

5 tbsp dry white wine
5 tbsp white wine vinegar
2 shallots, finely chopped
4 tbsp chopped fresh tarragon
10 peppercorns, crushed
4 egg yolks
250g (8oz) unsalted butter, clarified (see page 35) then cooled to room temperature, or chilled and cubed
1 tbsp chopped fresh chervil (optional)
2 tbsp lemon juice

1 Put the wine, vinegar, shallots, 2 tablespoons of the tarragon and the peppercorns in a small pan. Boil until reduced by half. Remove from the heat and allow to cool.

2 Strain the reduction through a sieve into a stainless steel or glass bowl. Place the bowl over a pan of just-simmering water, making sure that the base of the bowl does not touch the water. Add the egg yolks and whisk until they thicken and become smooth and creamy, about 5–8 minutes. Do not allow the mixture to get hotter than hand-hot or the eggs will coagulate.

3 If using clarified butter, pour it in slowly, whisking continuously, until the sauce is thick and fluffy. If you are using chilled, cubed butter, add a few pieces at a time, whisking continuously to ensure it is fully blended in. Stir in the remaining tarragon, the chervil, if using, and the lemon juice. Serve immediately.

BEURRE BLANC

3 shallots, finely chopped
3 tbsp white wine vinegar
150ml (¼ pint) dry white wine or water
250g (8oz) unsalted butter, chilled and cubed
a few drops of lemon juice
salt and freshly ground black pepper

A rich accompaniment to fish, beurre blanc, or butter sauce, is light, delicious and extremely calorific. It is very easy to make if you remember that, like custard, it should never be allowed to boil. This butter emulsion does not contain egg yolks.

1 Combine the shallots and vinegar in a small pan and bring to the boil. Cook over a medium heat until most of the vinegar has evaporated, then add the wine or water and boil until reduced by half.

2 Over a low heat, add the butter one piece at a time, whisking continuously to ensure that it blends into the sauce between each addition. When all the butter has been amalgamated, whisk in the lemon juice, season with salt and pepper and serve immediately.

VARIATIONS

ORANGE BUTTER SAUCE
Another favourite with fish; I like to serve this with salmon or cod. Follow the recipe above but reduce the wine or water to 100ml (3½fl oz) and add 60ml (2fl oz) orange juice.

LEMONGRASS BUTTER SAUCE *See page 13 for illustration*
My version of a Thai butter sauce, this marries well with delicately flavoured fish such as trout and salmon. Follow the recipe above, but use 160g (5½oz) chilled and cubed butter and 90g (3oz) chilled and cubed Lemongrass and Lime Butter (see page 74).

CHILLI BUTTER SAUCE
Serve this piquant butter sauce with fish, chicken or vegetables. Follow the recipe above but use 125g (4oz) chilled and cubed butter and 125g (4oz) chilled and cubed Chilli Butter (see page 74).

MALTAISE ▷

This is particularly good with poached salmon.

Advance preparation: the reduction (step 1) can be made in advance

100ml (3½fl oz) blood orange juice or ordinary orange juice
zest of 1 orange, thinly pared and cut into fine julienne
1 quantity of Hollandaise (see pages 34–35)

1 In a small pan simmer the orange juice until it has reduced by a third. In another pan blanch the orange zest in boiling water for 1 minute, then drain, refresh in cold water and drain again. Add the blanched zest to the orange juice reduction and bubble gently for 1 minute.

2 Stir the orange juice reduction into the Hollandaise just before serving.

EXOTIC HOLLANDAISE

Sharp, light and refreshing, this sauce is especially suitable for firm-fleshed fish such as tuna and swordfish or barramundi.

Advance preparation: the reduction (step 1) can be made in advance

100ml (3½fl oz) dry white wine or Fish Stock (see page 30)
2 lemongrass stalks, hard outer layers removed, finely chopped
50g (1¾oz) shallots, finely chopped
1cm (½ inch) fresh ginger, finely chopped
1 quantity of Hollandaise, made without the lemon juice (see pages 34–35)
2 tbsp lime juice
½ tsp grated lime zest
3 kaffir lime leaves, finely shredded (optional)
½ tsp chopped fresh red chilli or freshly ground black pepper
salt

1 Put the wine or stock, lemongrass, shallots and ginger in a small pan and boil until reduced by half. Remove from the heat and allow to cool.

2 Strain the reduction into a stainless steel or glass bowl. Finish as for Béarnaise Sauce (opposite) from step 2 but stir in the lime juice, zest, lime leaves, if using, and chilli instead of the herbs and lemon juice. Season with salt and serve.

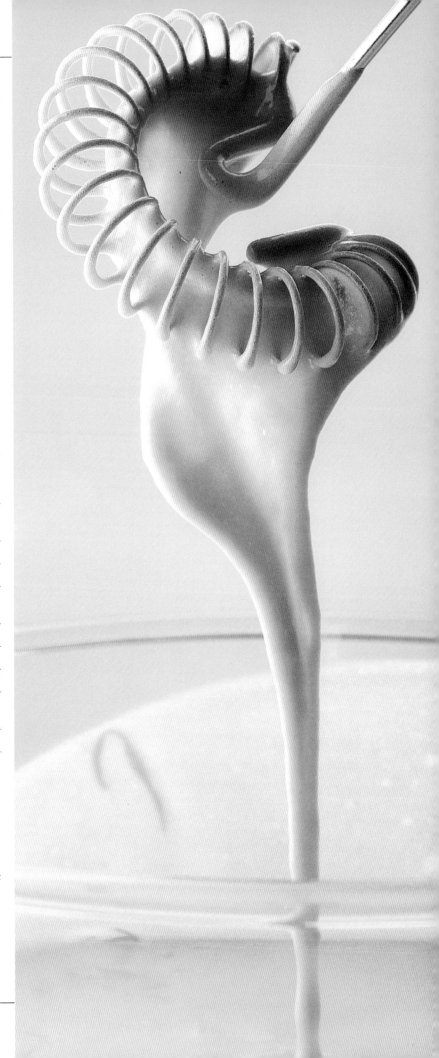

RIGHT: ORANGE JUICE GIVES MALTAISE A DELICATE ORANGE HUE

SABAYONS

LIGHT, FLUFFY AND DELICATELY FLAVOURED, sabayons are very easy to make and yet always look impressive. After mastering the technique (see master recipe, pages 36–37), you can create your own variations. The golden rule to remember is the proportion of 100ml (3½fl oz) liquid to 4 egg yolks. Up to 75g (2½oz) clarified butter (see page 35) can be beaten into the sauce before serving to create a richer but less fluffy sabayon.

◁ PINK CHAMPAGNE SABAYON

Perfect as a light and delicately flavoured accompaniment to poached shellfish or grilled lobster.

4 egg yolks

2 tbsp champagne vinegar or white wine vinegar

90ml (3 fl oz) pink champagne

salt and freshly ground black pepper

1 Place the egg yolks in a bowl, add the vinegar and beat either by hand or with an electric whisk until the mixture has turned slightly paler. Add the champagne and whisk well.

2 Place the bowl over a pan of just-simmering water, making sure the base of the bowl does not touch the water, and continue whisking for 8–10 minutes, until the sauce is thick and frothy. Season to taste and serve immediately.

VARIATION

SEAFOOD SABAYON

Follow the recipe above but use only 1 tablespoon of white wine vinegar and substitute 2 tablespoons of Ricard and 100ml (3½ fl oz) of Fish Stock (see page 30) for the champagne.

AVGOLEMONO

This classic Greek sauce is slightly sharp in flavour and goes particularly well with poached or roast chicken, or over steamed vegetables.

Advance preparation: *the chicken stock can be made in advance*

125ml (4fl oz) Chicken Stock (see page 28)

2 tsp arrowroot

strained juice of 3 lemons

grated zest of 1 lemon

3 egg yolks, well beaten

salt and freshly ground black pepper

1 Bring the chicken stock to the boil in a small non-corrosive pan. Dissolve the arrowroot in 2 tablespoons of the lemon juice and add to the stock with the remaining lemon juice and the zest. Stirring well, bring the sauce back to the boil.

2 Reduce the heat and add the egg yolks in a thin, steady stream, beating continuously. Go on beating for 1–2 minutes until the sauce thickens slightly. Remove from the heat, season to taste and serve immediately.

ORANGE & SAFFRON SABAYON

strained juice of 2 oranges

200ml (7 fl oz) Chicken or Fish Stock (see pages 28 and 30)

½ tsp coriander seeds, dry-roasted and crushed (see page 78)

½ tsp saffron strands, soaked in 2 tbsp warmed brandy

4 egg yolks

1 tbsp lemon juice

grated zest of ½ orange

salt and freshly ground black pepper

Elegant, frothy, flavoursome and brilliantly coloured, this sabayon is wonderful served with chicken or fish.

Advance preparation: the reduction (step 1) can be made in advance

1 Put the orange juice, stock, coriander seeds and saffron mixture in a small pan and boil rapidly until approximately 100ml (3½ fl oz) is left. Remove from the heat and allow to cool.

2 Place the egg yolks in a bowl, add the cooled reduction and the lemon juice and beat, either by hand or with an electric whisk, until the mixture has turned slightly paler.

3 Place the bowl over a pan of just-simmering water, making sure the water does not touch the base of the bowl. Whisk until the sauce is thick and frothy, about 8–10 minutes. Add the orange zest, season and serve immediately.

COULIS

IN FRENCH, THE WORD *COULIS* refers to a thin purée of fish, poultry or vegetables often used to thicken soups and stews. In modern cookery it means raw or cooked fruit or vegetable purées that are diluted to a pouring consistency with stock, wine or, in the case of sweet coulis, sugar syrup. Coulis are wonderful in their simplicity – once you have mastered the technique, experiment with different vegetables, herbs and fruit.

WATERCRESS COULIS

A marvellous accompaniment to fish or cooked vegetables.

Advance preparation: the stock can be made in advance

3 bunches of watercress, leaves and stems separated, stems of 1 bunch chopped and reserved

300ml (½ pint) Fish or Chicken Stock (see pages 30 and 28) or white wine

50g (1¾oz) shallots, finely chopped

2 garlic cloves, finely chopped

a bouquet garni made with 4 sprigs of mint, 1 strip of lemon zest and 1 sprig of lemon thyme (see page 30)

2–3 tbsp crème fraîche (optional)

lemon juice to taste

salt and freshly ground black pepper

1 Bring a pan of water to the boil and plunge in the watercress leaves. When the water reaches the boil again, remove the pan from the heat, drain the leaves and refresh them immediately in iced water. Drain the leaves again and squeeze out the remaining water.

2 Pour the stock or wine into a small pan, add the shallots, garlic, watercress stems and bouquet garni and bring to the boil. Reduce the heat and simmer gently until the liquid has reduced by half. Strain and reserve the liquid, discarding the vegetables.

3 Place the blanched watercress leaves and the strained reduction in a food processor or blender and process until smooth and creamy. For smoother results, sieve the sauce after blending.

4 Return to a clean pan and heat very gently. Mix in the crème fraîche, if using, and heat for 1 minute, without letting the sauce boil. Season to taste and add the lemon juice just before serving.

CARROT COULIS

6 tbsp olive or groundnut oil

1 tsp turmeric

1 tsp coriander seeds, freshly ground

350g (11½oz) carrots, chopped

1 tbsp good honey

400ml (14fl oz) Chicken or Vegetable Stock (see pages 28 and 31) or dry white wine

2 tbsp chopped fresh coriander

¼ tsp chilli powder

2–3 tbsp lemon juice

finely grated lemon zest to taste (optional)

salt

A bright orange coulis with a spicy curry flavour that goes very well with cooked vegetables such as cauliflower and broccoli.

Advance preparation: the stock can be made in advance

Shelf-life: 1 week in the refrigerator if made without the oil and lemon

1 Heat 4 tablespoons of the oil in a pan, add the turmeric and ground coriander and fry for 1 minute. Add the carrots and honey and continue to fry until the carrots start to colour, about 8 minutes.

2 Add the stock or wine, bring to the boil and simmer for about 30 minutes, or until the carrots are very tender and the cooking liquid has reduced by about half.

3 Transfer the carrot mixture to a blender or food processor and whizz to a smooth and creamy consistency.

4 Return to a clean pan and heat to boiling point. Remove from the heat, add the fresh coriander and chilli powder and season with salt. Beat in the remaining 2 tablespoons of oil with the lemon juice and the zest, if using. If a thinner consistency is preferred, stir in 1–2 tablespoons of stock or water.

AVOCADO COULIS

A creamy, smooth, piquant sauce that can be served either hot or cold. It is particularly good with oily fish but also makes a surprisingly delicious pasta sauce.

Advance preparation: the stock can be made in advance

400ml (14fl oz) Chicken Stock (see page 28)

75g (2½oz) shallots, finely chopped

1 small, ripe avocado, halved and flesh scooped out

2 tbsp lime juice

finely grated lime zest to taste

1 small red chilli, deseeded and finely chopped

3 tbsp double cream

salt

---

1 Put the stock and shallots in a small pan, bring to the boil, then reduce the heat and simmer until reduced by half. Remove from the heat and set aside to cool.

2 Place the avocado flesh in a blender or food processor, add the cooled stock reduction and the lime juice and process to a smooth cream.

3 Transfer the mixture to a small pan and slowly heat to just below boiling point. Add the lime zest and chilli and heat for a further minute. Remove from the heat, add salt to taste and beat in the cream.

FRESH TOMATO COULIS

Wonderfully versatile, this coulis can be served as a dip, used to add freshness to grilled fish or meat, or poured over pasta. It can also be flavoured with thyme or lemon thyme.

Advance preparation: the tomato pureé can be made in advance

Shelf-life: 3 days in the refrigerator

See page 17 for illustration

---

1 quantity of Tomato Purée (see page 43)

2 tbsp lemon juice

5–6 tbsp extra-virgin olive oil or cold-pressed hazelnut oil

2 tbsp chopped fresh basil, mint, flat-leaf parsley or coriander

salt and freshly ground black pepper

---

1 Place the purée in a deep bowl and whisk in the lemon juice. Whisk in the oil a spoonful at a time.

2 Add the herbs, season to taste and mix well. Chill before serving.

COOKED TOMATO COULIS

5 tbsp olive oil

100g (3½oz) shallots, finely chopped

3 garlic cloves, crushed

1kg (2lb) cooking tomatoes (plum, beef or marmande), peeled, deseeded and chopped (see page 43)

a bouquet garni made with a few sprigs of thyme, 1 sprig of rosemary, a few celery leaves, 1 bay leaf and 1 strip of lemon zest (see page 30)

1 tsp sugar or honey (optional)

2 tbsp chopped fresh basil, mint, oregano or parsley (optional)

salt

freshly ground black pepper or 1 small red or green chilli, chopped

---

1 Heat 3 tablespoons of the olive oil in a frying pan, add the shallots and garlic and fry gently until the shallots are translucent, about 5 minutes.

2 Add the tomatoes and the bouquet garni and simmer over a low heat for about 1 hour, stirring from time to time, until all the moisture has evaporated. Add the sugar or honey, if using.

3 Remove the bouquet garni, transfer the sauce to a blender or food processor and process until smooth.

4 Return the sauce to a clean pan and heat to boiling point, then remove from the heat and season to taste. Add the herbs, if using, and beat in the remaining 2 tablespoons of oil.

A simple and delicious tomato sauce that can be served as an accompaniment to vegetable dishes, grilled meat or fish, or tossed with pasta. Add a teaspoon of sugar or honey to enhance the tomatoes if they are a little bland. For extra flavour, beat in a little more olive oil just before serving. This sauce is so useful that it is worth making a larger quantity and storing it for future use.

Shelf-life: 1 week in the refrigerator; 3 months in the freezer

REDUCTION SAUCES

REDUCTION SAUCES are simply sauces based on stock that has been reduced by boiling to give an intense flavour. The classic reduction sauce is demi-glace, which is worth mastering because it can form the base of many other wonderful sauces. One of the essential *haute cuisine* sauces, it can take as long as two days to prepare because you need to make a good stock first. Although the process can be time consuming, the results always justify the bother, as a faithfully reduced sauce will be well-rounded, robust and extremely flavoursome.

DEMI-GLACE

THIS LIGHTER AND HEALTHIER VERSION of the conventional demi-glace uses no flour or Madeira, yet the finished sauce is clear, robust and rich and can be served with red meat or used as a base for other sauces. Adding butter at the end gives the demi-glace a wonderful rich gloss, but omit this and the seasoning if using the demi-glace as a base for other sauces.

To save a little time, roughly chop the vegetables in a food processor rather than by hand. See opposite for richer, more conventional demi-glace recipes.

Makes 250–300ml (8fl oz–½pint)

2 tbsp olive oil

30g (1oz) butter

150g (5oz) shallots, finely chopped

200g (7oz) carrots, finely chopped

100g (3½oz) celery, finely chopped

100g (3½oz) leek, white part only, finely chopped

150g (5oz) very ripe tomatoes, peeled, deseeded and chopped (see page 43)

a bouquet garni made with 2 green leek leaves, 3 sprigs thyme, 1 sprig rosemary, a few sprigs parsley and 1 bay leaf (see page 30)

1.5 litres (2½ pints) Brown Veal or Chicken Stock (see pages 29 and 28)

30g (1oz) butter, chilled and cubed (optional)

salt, if necessary, and freshly ground black pepper (optional)

Shelf-life: 1 week in the refrigerator

1 Heat the olive oil and butter in a large pan, add the shallots, carrots, celery and leek and fry gently until lightly browned and caramelized.

2 Add the tomatoes, bouquet garni and stock and bring to the boil. Reduce the heat and simmer, regularly skimming any residue from the surface, until reduced by a third, about 45–50 minutes.

3 Strain the reduction through a fine sieve or a sieve lined with muslin. Transfer to a clean pan. Simmer the strained reduction for 45 minutes–1 hour, or until reduced by about three quarters.

4 The finished demi-glace should be thick and syrupy in consistency and evenly coat the back of a spoon. If the demi-glace is to be served as a sauce, whisk in the butter a little at a time, then season to taste.

MADEIRA DEMI-GLACE

This is a richer version of the demi-glace.

Advance preparation: the demi-glace can be made in advance

Shelf-life: 1 week in the refrigerator, although it is best served fresh

| 1 quantity of Demi-glace (see opposite) |
| 100ml (3½fl oz) Madeira |
| 30g (1oz) butter, chilled and cubed |
| salt and freshly ground black pepper |

1. Bring the demi-glace and the Madeira slowly to the boil in a small pan. Reduce the heat to minimum and simmer, skimming any residue from the surface, until it has reduced by a third.

2. Remove from the heat, season to taste and whisk in the butter a little at a time.

VARIATION

RED DEMI-GLACE
This is a decadent and wonderfully rich sauce that makes the perfect accompaniment to grilled steak.
• Bring 1 quantity of Demi-glace (see opposite) to the boil and add 200ml (7fl oz) good, full-bodied red wine, such as Rioja, Shiraz or Merlot. Reduce the heat to minimum and add 3 sprigs of fresh thyme.
• Simmer, skimming any residue from the surface, until it has reduced by half, about 30 minutes. Strain, season and finish by whisking in 30g (1oz) of chilled and cubed butter a little at a time as in the demi-glace recipe.

JUNIPER DEMI-GLACE

Robust and full of Mediterranean flavour, this sauce goes particularly well with pink roast lamb.

Advance preparation: the demi-glace can be made in advance

Shelf-life: 1 week in the refrigerator

See page 21 for illustration

| 1 quantity of Demi-glace (see opposite) |
| 200ml (7fl oz) good, full-bodied red wine such as Rioja, Shiraz or Merlot |
| 1 tbsp gin |
| 2 small sprigs rosemary |
| 10 juniper berries, crushed |
| 30g (1oz) butter, chilled and cubed |
| salt and freshly ground black pepper |

1 Bring the demi-glace, wine and gin to the boil in a pan. Reduce the heat and add the rosemary and juniper berries. Simmer, skimming any scum from the surface, until it has reduced by half.

2 Strain into a clean pan and bring back to the boil, then remove from the heat. Season and gradually whisk in the butter.

THICKENED DEMI-GLACE

| 60g (2oz) clarified butter (see page 35) |
| 150g (5oz) shallots, finely chopped |
| 200g (7oz) carrots, finely chopped |
| 100g (3½oz) celery, finely chopped |
| 100g (3½oz) leek, white part only, finely chopped |
| 2–3 tbsp plain flour, sifted |
| 2 litres (3½ pints) Brown Veal or Chicken Stock (see pages 29 and 28) |
| 150g (5oz) very red tomatoes, peeled, deseeded and chopped (see page 43) |
| a bouquet garni made with 2 green leek leaves, 3 sprigs of thyme, 1 sprig of rosemary, a few sprigs of parsley and 1 bay leaf (see page 30) |
| strained lemon juice to taste |
| salt and freshly ground black pepper |

This is easier and relatively quicker to prepare than the modern Demi-glace (see opposite). It is thickened with flour and therefore the reduction does not take as long. Although robust, this sauce does not have the intense flavour of the demi-glace. Use instead of demi-glace as a base for other sauces.

Advance preparation: the stock can be made in advance

1 Heat the butter in a large pan, add the shallots, carrots, celery and leek and fry gently until lightly browned, about 10–15 minutes. Sprinkle with the flour and fry, stirring continuously, until the flour starts to brown, about 5–8 minutes.

2 Add the stock and, stirring, bring to the boil, skimming any residue from the surface when necessary. Add the tomatoes and the bouquet garni and simmer until the stock has reduced by two thirds.

3 Strain through a fine sieve or a sieve lined with muslin. Season with salt and pepper and finish with a few drops of lemon juice.

WILD MUSHROOM DEMI-GLACE

This is a wonderfully hearty and rich sauce that is perfect with steak.

Advance preparation: the demi-glace can be made in advance

Shelf-life: 1 week in the refrigerator if made without the butter

15g (½oz) dried porcini, soaked in 75ml (2½fl oz) hot water for 30 minutes

1 quantity of Demi-glace (see page 60)

200ml (7fl oz) good red wine

2 sprigs of fresh thyme

1 fat garlic clove, finely chopped

30g (1oz) butter, chilled and cubed

salt and freshly ground black pepper

1 Drain the porcini, reserving the soaking liquid, and chop finely. Put the demi-glace, wine and the strained porcini soaking liquid in a pan and slowly bring to the boil. Reduce the heat to minimum and add the porcini, thyme and garlic. Simmer, skimming any scum from the surface when necessary, until it has reduced by half.

2 Strain into a clean pan and bring back to the boil. Switch off the heat, season, and whisk in the butter a little at a time.

RED WINE SAUCE

This sauce of Eastern European origin is especially good with poached or fried carp. It also goes well with salmon and bass and with freshwater fish such as trout and tilapia.

Advance preparation: the stock can be made in advance

Shelf-life: 1 week in the refrigerator if made without the butter

1 tbsp light olive oil or groundnut oil

75g (2½oz) shallot, finely chopped

75g (2½oz) carrot, finely chopped

2.5cm (1 inch) fresh ginger, shredded

1 tbsp good honey

500ml (17fl oz) Fish Stock made with red wine (see page 30)

300ml (½ pint) fruity red wine

2 tsp sweet Hungarian paprika

¼ tsp hot Hungarian paprika or cayenne pepper

lemon juice to taste

¼ tsp grated lemon zest

75g (2½oz) butter, chilled and cubed

salt and freshly ground black pepper

1 Heat the oil in a small pan, add the shallot, carrot, ginger and honey and fry, stirring frequently, until the shallot turns golden and begins to caramelize. Add the stock and wine and bring to the boil, then reduce the heat and bubble gently, skimming any scum from the surface when necessary, until the sauce has reduced by two thirds, about 25 minutes.

2 Strain the sauce through a fine sieve into a clean pan, add the sweet paprika and the hot paprika or cayenne pepper, and bring to the boil. Reduce the heat and allow to bubble for 10 minutes.

3 Season to taste and add the lemon juice and zest. Remove from the heat and whisk in the butter a little at a time just before serving.

ORANGE & SAFFRON SAUCE ▷

strained juice of 3 oranges

400ml (14fl oz) Fish Stock (see page 30)

¼ tsp saffron strands, soaked in a little warm fish stock or water

½ tsp arrowroot, dissolved in 1 tbsp orange juice or water

thinly pared zest of 1 orange, cut into fine julienne

a few drops of lemon juice

½ tsp finely chopped red chilli or ½ tsp cayenne pepper

75g (2½oz) butter, chilled and cubed

salt

A superbly fragrant sauce that is especially good with strong-flavoured fish, such as red or grey mullet or tuna.

Advance preparation: the stock can be made in advance

Shelf-life: 3–4 days in the refrigerator if made without the butter

1 Place the orange juice and stock in a pan and bring to the boil. Reduce the heat and simmer gently, skimming any residue from the surface when necessary, until it has reduced by two thirds, about 25 minutes.

2 Add the saffron, arrowroot and orange zest and whisk for about a minute until the sauce has thickened slightly. Add the lemon juice and chilli or cayenne. Simmer for 2 minutes, then remove from the heat, whisk in the butter a little at a time, season with salt and serve immediately.

OPPOSITE: RED MULLET IN A TANGY ORANGE AND SAFFRON SAUCE GARNISHED WITH A SPRIG OF ROSEMARY

GINGER & SPRING ONION SAUCE

An interesting marriage of East and West, this piquant sauce is especially good with salmon.

Advance preparation: the stock can be made in advance

Shelf-life: 3 days in the refrigerator if made without the butter

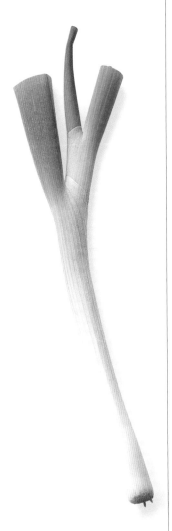

125g (4oz) spring onions
30g (1 oz) butter
1 tbsp plain flour
1 tbsp Cooked Tomato Coulis (see page 59) or 1 tsp Tomato Purée (see page 43) or 1 tsp bought tomato purée
400ml (14 fl oz) Fish Stock (see page 30)
1cm (½ inch) fresh ginger, finely shredded
2 tbsp lemon juice
cayenne pepper to taste
75g (2½oz) butter, chilled and cubed
salt

1 Finely chop the white part of the spring onions. Snip 4 or 5 of the tender green tops into pieces and set aside.

2 Heat the butter in a small pan, add the chopped spring onions and fry gently until they begin to colour. Sprinkle in the flour and fry for 2 minutes, then add the tomato coulis or purée and cook for a minute or so, stirring frequently.

3 Add the stock, whisking to incorporate any bits from the bottom of the pan, and bring to the boil. Reduce the heat and simmer gently, skimming any scum from the surface when necessary, until the sauce has reduced by half, about 25 minutes. Whisk often to prevent sticking.

4 Pass the sauce through a sieve into a clean pan, using the back of a spoon to push through as much of the onion as possible. Add the ginger and simmer for 1–2 minutes, then remove from the heat and add the lemon juice. Season with cayenne pepper and salt to taste. Beat in the butter a few pieces at a time, add the snipped spring onion tops and serve immediately.

LEMON SAUCE

400ml (14 fl oz) Fish Stock (see page 30)
strained juice and finely grated zest of 1 small lemon
½ tsp sugar or honey
1 tsp arrowroot, dissolved in 1 tbsp white wine or water
½ or 1 small preserved lemon, rinsed, pulp removed and skin finely chopped
1 small red chilli, chopped (optional)
100g (3½oz) butter, chilled and cubed
salt and freshly ground black pepper

1 Put the stock, lemon juice and sugar or honey in a pan and bring to the boil. Reduce the heat and bubble very gently, skimming any scum from the surface when necessary, until reduced by two thirds.

2 Add the arrowroot and stir until the mixture has thickened slightly. Add the lemon zest and the preserved lemon and the chilli, if using, and bubble for 2–3 minutes. Remove from the heat, beat in the butter a little at a time, then season to taste.

Moroccan preserved lemon lends this refreshing sauce a delightfully tart, piquant flavour. It is especially good with grilled red mullet or grilled oily fish such as mackerel, but if you substitute chicken stock for the fish stock it also makes a good sauce for chicken. Preserved lemons are available in Middle Eastern and Mediterranean shops.

Advance preparation: the stock can be made in advance

Shelf-life: 1 week in the refrigerator if made without the butter

BALSAMIC VINEGAR SAUCE

400ml (14 fl oz) Fish Stock, made with red wine (see page 30)
100ml (3½ fl oz) 10–15-year-old balsamic vinegar
1 tsp arrowroot, dissolved in 1 tbsp balsamic vinegar
100g (3½oz) butter, chilled and cubed
salt and freshly ground black pepper

Simple and quick, this sauce makes a memorable dish when served with salmon, trout or sea bass.

Advance preparation: the stock can be made in advance

Shelf-life: 1 week in the refrigerator if made without the butter

1 Bring the stock and balsamic vinegar to the boil in a small pan. Reduce the heat and bubble gently for 15–20 minutes, skimming any scum from the surface when necessary, until reduced by two thirds.

2 Increase the heat, add the arrowroot and boil for 1 minute until thickened. Whisk in the butter a little at a time, then season to taste with salt and freshly ground black pepper. Serve immediately.

GRAVIES

THE WORD GRAVY comes via France from a Latin word meaning made with grain. It describes a particularly British sauce made by thickening and deglazing pan juices after roasting meat. A lighter, more contemporary gravy can be made by omitting the flour and simmering for a few minutes longer. It is important to make the sauce in a roasting pan as its large surface area helps the process of evaporation and thickening.

TRADITIONAL PAN GRAVY

This is made from the pan juices left behind after cooking a roast.

Advance preparation: the stock can be made in advance

Shelf-life: 1 week in the refrigerator

1–2 tbsp plain flour or ½–1 tbsp cornflour

500ml (17fl oz) Brown or Chicken Stock (see pages 29 and 28) or ½ red or white wine and ½ stock

2–3 tbsp chopped fresh parsley (optional)

salt and freshly ground black pepper

1 Remove the roast meat or poultry from the roasting pan and leave to rest in a warm place. Drain off all but 2 tablespoons of the fat that will have collected in the bottom of the pan.

2 Place the roasting pan on top of the stove over a low heat and sprinkle in the flour or cornflour. Cook for 3–4 minutes, stirring continuously and scraping any residue from the base of the pan.

3 Add the stock and bring to the boil, stirring, then simmer for about 5–8 minutes, until the gravy has thickened slightly. Season, add the parsley, if using, and serve in a sauceboat with the meat.

VARIATIONS

GRAVY FOR LAMB OR GAME
Follow the recipe above but use 350ml (12fl oz) stock and 150ml (¼ pint) port.

TOMATO GRAVY *See page 17 for illustration*
Follow the recipe for Traditional Pan Gravy but add 75g (2½oz) chopped sun-dried tomatoes and 1 tablespoon Tomato Purée (see page 43) or shop-bought tomato purée just before adding the flour. Serve with roast lamb or chicken.

MUSTARD GRAVY
Follow the recipe for Traditional Pan Gravy but, before serving, stir in 1 heaped tablespoon grainy mustard. Serve with chicken.

ONION GRAVY

60g (2oz) butter or bacon fat

500g (1lb) onions, halved and sliced paper-thin

1 tbsp plain flour

750ml (1¼ pints) Brown Stock (see page 29)

1 tbsp lemon juice

¼ tsp cayenne pepper or a few drops of Tabasco sauce

salt and freshly ground black pepper

One of the magic sauces of British cuisine, this sweet and comforting gravy is especially good with sausages, or just poured over mashed potatoes, roasted meat or poultry.

Advance preparation: the stock can be made in advance

Shelf-life: 1 week in the refrigerator

1 Heat the butter or bacon fat in a pan, add the onions and sweat over a medium heat until they are soft and translucent, about 10–15 minutes.

2 Sprinkle with the flour and cook for about 3 minutes, scraping the base of the pan and stirring continuously.

3 Add the stock and bring to the boil, then reduce the heat and simmer until reduced by half. Add the lemon juice and the cayenne pepper or Tabasco, season to taste and serve.

VARIATION

CARAMELIZED ONION GRAVY
For a sweeter, richer, more intensely flavoured onion gravy, follow the recipe above but cook the onions for 40–50 minutes, or until evenly browned and jam-like. Finish as from Step 2, above.

DRESSINGS

HERE IS AN INSPIRATIONAL COLLECTION OF RECIPES THAT ARE BOTH EASY AND FUN TO PREPARE, GATHERED

FROM ALL CORNERS OF THE WORLD. THESE DRESSINGS CAN BE DRIZZLED OVER SALADS BUT THEIR FLAVOURS

AND SIMPLICITY MAKE THEM VERSATILE: TRY USING THEM IN SANDWICHES INSTEAD OF BUTTER, SPOONING THEM

OVER STEAMED OR BOILED VEGETABLES OR POURING THEM OVER GRILLED MEAT OR FISH.

BLUE CHEESE DRESSING

For a less calorific version use 150ml (5fl oz) low-fat or fat-free Greek-style yogurt instead of the mayonnaise.

Advance preparation: *the mayonnaise can be made in advance*

Shelf-life: *1 week in the refrigerator*

1 quantity of Mayonnaise
(see pages 38–39)

150g (5oz) blue cheese, such as Danish blue, gorgonzola or dolcelatte, crumbled

2 tbsp white wine vinegar

salt, if necessary, and freshly ground black pepper

Place all the ingredients in a food processor and process until smooth.

THOUSAND ISLAND DRESSING

One of the more famous salad dressings, this can also be served over hard-boiled eggs or as a dip for crudités. If using tomato ketchup, remember to spike the sauce with a pinch of cayenne, chilli powder or a few drops of Tabasco.

Advance preparation: *the mayonnaise can be made in advance*

Shelf-life: *1 week in the refrigerator*

1 quantity of Mayonnaise
(see pages 38–39)

4 tbsp mild chilli sauce or tomato ketchup

1 hard-boiled egg, finely chopped

2 tbsp finely chopped stuffed green olives

1 tbsp finely chopped onion

1 tbsp finely chopped green pepper

1 tbsp finely chopped sour gherkin

1 tbsp snipped fresh chives

1 tbsp lemon or lime juice

salt and freshly ground black pepper

Mix all the ingredients together in a bowl.

FETA CHEESE DRESSING

100g (3 ½oz) feta cheese

2 tbsp lemon juice

1 garlic clove, crushed

1 tsp grated lemon zest

4 tbsp extra-virgin olive oil

3 tbsp chopped fresh mint or flat-leaf parsley

freshly ground black pepper

Creamy, sharp and delicious, this dressing goes particularly well with tomato and onion salad, but can also be served as a dip or poured over rice or pasta.

Shelf-life: *1 week in the refrigerator*

Place all the ingredients except the mint or parsley in a food processor and process until smooth. Add the mint or parsley and process briefly to mix.

MANGO DRESSING ▷

1 ripe mango, peeled and stoned

juice of 2 limes or 1 lemon

1 tbsp Dijon or English mustard

1 tsp grated lemon or lime zest

1 small chilli, deseeded and finely chopped

2 tbsp snipped fresh chives

salt and freshly ground black pepper

A delicious fat-free dressing that can be served over a green salad or as a sauce for grilled fish or meat. Add a little sugar if necessary to balance the flavours. Stirring in the zest, chilli and chives at the end keeps the textured consistency.

Shelf-life: *1 week in the refrigerator*

Process the mango flesh and lime or lemon juice in a food processor until smooth. If the mango is stringy, pass the purée through a fine sieve. Transfer to a bowl and stir in the remaining ingredients.

OPPOSITE: SNIPPED FRESH CHIVES BEING STIRRED INTO MANGO DRESSING

SOURED CREAM DRESSING

This is a popular topping for baked potatoes and green salads. For a low-calorie version substitute low-fat or fat-free Greek-style yogurt for the soured cream.

Shelf-life: *1 week in the refrigerator*

150ml (¼ pint) thick soured cream or fromage frais
1–2 tbsp lemon juice, white wine vinegar or cider vinegar
1 tsp Dijon mustard (optional)
2 tbsp snipped fresh chives, dill or flat-leaf parsley
salt and freshly ground white or black pepper

Mix all the ingredients together in a bowl.

TAHINI SAUCE

A versatile Middle Eastern sauce that is served as a dip with pitta bread or as a salad dressing. For a richer flavour, mix in 2–3 tablespoons of extra-virgin olive oil just before serving. To use this as a cooking sauce, add 250ml (8fl oz) milk or water, then pour over cooked vegetables or grilled or fried fish and bake or grill until golden.

Shelf-life: *1 week in the refrigerator (omit the garlic and add just before serving)*

250g (8oz) tahini
strained juice of 2 lemons or to taste
175ml (6fl oz) water
1 garlic clove, crushed (optional)
2–3 tbsp chopped fresh flat-leaf parsley or mint (optional)
salt

1 Mix the tahini and lemon juice together in a small bowl. The mixture will separate and may appear lumpy at first, but continue to mix, adding small quantities of the water, and it will soon reach the consistency of double cream.

2 Add the rest of the ingredients and mix well. Alternatively, put all the ingredients except the herbs, if using, in a food processor and process to a smooth cream. Add the herbs.

VARIATIONS

HAZELNUT OR PEANUT TAHINI
Follow the recipe above, but substitute 200g (7oz) hazelnut butter (available from healthfood shops) or peanut butter for the tahini.

GREEN TAHINI
This is a bright green, fresh-tasting version of tahini that can be made in a food processor or blender. Make the tahini sauce as above but omit the parsley or mint. Process 100g (3½oz) fresh flat-leaf parsley, mint or dill, or a mixture of all three, with 3 tablespoons of tahini sauce until smooth, 1–2 minutes. With the machine running, add the remaining tahini sauce and process to blend.

SALAD CREAM

1 tbsp mustard powder
2 tbsp plain flour or cornflour
1–2 tbsp caster sugar or to taste
3 egg yolks
250ml (8fl oz) single cream, double cream or milk
100ml (3½fl oz) cider vinegar or white wine vinegar
salt

Favoured by children of all ages, this classic British sauce is easy to make, has less fat then mayonnaise and keeps very well. As when making custard, salad cream should be stirred continuously and never allowed to boil. The finished sauce can be bottled and stored.

Shelf-life: *1 week in the refrigerator; 2 weeks in a sealed jar (see pages 134–35)*

1 Mix the mustard, flour, sugar and egg yolks together in a bowl. Gradually add the cream or milk, beating well.

2 Place the bowl over a pan of just-simmering water, making sure the base of the bowl does not touch the water, and stir until it starts to thicken. Add the vinegar and salt and cook until thick and smooth.

VINAIGRETTE

2 tsp Dijon mustard
1 tablespoon honey (optional)
2 tbsp wine vinegar, cider vinegar or other flavoured vinegar, or lemon or lime juice
6–8 tbsp good olive oil
salt and freshly ground black pepper

Vinaigrette is one of the simplest and most versatile sauces. Use it to dress salads or add succulence to dry, cured meats, or pour it over grilled or fried fish as a sauce. I like to drizzle it over pasta, burghul, couscous or rice for a fast yet satisfying meal.

Shelf-life: *3 weeks refrigerated in a screw-top jar*

In a bowl, whisk together the mustard, honey, vinegar or lemon or lime juice and seasoning. Gradually add the oil, whisking constantly, until the sauce is smooth and thick. Alternatively, put all the ingredients in a screw-top jar and shake well to mix.

VARIATIONS

ROQUEFORT DRESSING
I drizzle this over salads as well as grilled steak and lamb chops. Follow the recipe above but mix the vinaigrette in a blender or food processor and add 60g (2oz) crumbled Roquefort cheese.

GARLIC & HERB VINAIGRETTE
Follow the recipe above but add 1 crushed garlic clove and 1–2 tablespoons chopped fresh parsley, coriander, chives or tarragon.

PEPPER & CHILLI VINAIGRETTE

A vinaigrette for chilli lovers. You can also use tinned roasted peppers, which are widely available in supermarkets and at Mediterranean, Middle Eastern or South American delicatessens.

Shelf–life: *1 week in the refrigerator*

1 quantity of Vinaigrette made with lemon or lime juice (see opposite)

2 tbsp finely chopped roasted and peeled red pepper (see page 96)

½ tsp grated lemon or lime zest

1–2 green or red chillies, deseeded and finely chopped

1–2 tbsp chopped fresh coriander leaves

Mix all the ingredients together in a bowl.

COOKED VINAIGRETTE

This sauce is based on a recipe by Nico Ladenis, one of London's most innovative chefs. In the original recipe the vinaigrette is strained and the vegetables discarded. I like to leave the vegetables in the vinaigrette and serve it as a textured sauce with vegetables, fish or meat. It's not really worth making this in small quantities, especially since it keeps so well.

Makes 1.5 litres (2½ pints)

Shelf–life: *1 month in the refrigerator; 6 months in a sealed jar (see pages 134–35)*

See page 23 for illustration

1 litre (1¾ pints) olive oil

100ml (3½fl oz) white wine vinegar

1 tbsp good honey (optional)

350ml (12fl oz) dry white wine

100g (3½oz) carrots, finely chopped

100g (3½oz) celery, finely chopped

100g (3½oz) red pepper, finely chopped

100g (3½oz) shallots, finely chopped

5 garlic cloves, finely chopped

a bouquet garni made with 4 sprigs of thyme, 2 sprigs of rosemary, 2 strips of lemon zest and 2 bay leaves (see page 30)

1 tsp black peppercorns and ½ tsp cloves, tied in a muslin bag

150g (5oz) plum tomatoes, skinned, deseeded (see page 43) and finely chopped

1 tsp salt

1 Heat the oil, vinegar and honey, if using, in a pan. Add the rest of the ingredients and bring to the boil. Reduce the heat to minimum and simmer for about 30 minutes, skimming any scum from the surface when necessary.

2 Remove the bouquet garni and, if desired, strain through a muslin-lined sieve to remove the vegetables.

STEVE'S SPICY VINAIGRETTE

100ml (3½fl oz) fresh orange juice

strained juice of ½ lemon

6 tbsp olive oil

1 tbsp honey

1 tbsp Dijon mustard

1 tsp grated ginger

½ tsp grated orange zest

salt and freshly ground black pepper

This recipe was given to me by my good friend Steve. Spicy and intense in flavour, it makes a superb dressing for cooked or raw celeriac. It is also delicious with oily fish or as a simple sauce for grilled duck or game birds.

Shelf-life: *1 week in the refrigerator*

1 Simmer the orange and lemon juice in a small pan until reduced to about 3 tablespoons, then set aside to cool.

2 Transfer the cooled mixture to a bowl and whisk in the oil, honey and mustard. Mix in the ginger, orange zest and seasoning.

RASPBERRY VINAIGRETTE

2 tbsp raspberry vinegar or red wine vinegar

1 tsp honey

60g (2oz) fresh raspberries

6 tbsp olive or hazelnut oil

1 tbsp snipped fresh chervil or flat-leaf parsley

salt and freshly ground black pepper

Bright red, refreshing and tart, this is especially good, cold or warmed slightly, drizzled over duck or chicken salad, grilled goat's cheese, plain grilled poultry or oily fish.

Shelf-life: *1 week in the refrigerator*

See page 21 for illustration

Mix the vinegar and honey together in a bowl. Crush the raspberries to a pulp with a fork, then whisk them into the vinegar mixture along with the oil, chervil or parsley and seasoning.

WARM MAPLE VINAIGRETTE

3 tbsp cider vinegar

3 tbsp maple syrup

1 tsp made English mustard

8 tbsp olive or walnut oil

salt and freshly ground black pepper

A sweet and sour dressing that is excellent with grilled chicken or chicken salad, or just spooned over steamed vegetables.

Shelf-life: *1 week in the refrigerator*

Warm the vinegar and maple syrup in a small pan. Whisk in the mustard and the oil, season to taste and serve warm.

FLAVOURED OILS

A FEW DROPS OF FLAVOURED OIL in a stew or sauce can add instant fragrance and interest. Drizzle a couple of tablespoons over pasta and sprinkle with fresh herbs for a fast, convenient and delicious meal. Unless specified otherwise in the recipe, use light, well-filtered and refined oil, such as groundnut, sesame, vegetable or soy; cold-pressed virgin oils have a strong taste that might overpower more subtle flavourings. Oils that contain raw ingredients should be stored in sterilized jars (see pages 134–35).

HERB OIL

I use herb-flavoured oils in salad dressings or, added at the last minute, to flavour soups and stews. Try herbs such as basil, thyme and rosemary, and experiment with different combinations.

Shelf-life: 3 weeks unfiltered; 6 months filtered

See page 11 for illustration

| 1 litre (1¾ pints) good, light olive oil |
| 200g (7oz) fresh herb leaves |

Heat the oil to 40°C (104°F) in a pan. Lightly bruise the herbs, then put them in a sterilized jar or bottle (see pages 134–35). Pour the warm oil over the herbs and seal. Leave in a cool, dark place for 2–3 weeks, shaking the bottle occasionally. The oil is now ready for use but will last longer if it is filtered and the herbs discarded (see page 135).

VARIATION

LAVENDER OIL
Lavender is a wonderful, aromatic flavouring for oil. Add this oil to salad dressings or sauces, or drizzle it over steamed vegetables. Follow the recipe above, but use 1 litre (1¾ pints) almond or groundnut oil instead of olive oil. Substitute 200–300g (7–10oz) lavender flowerheads for the herbs.

THAI CARAMELIZED OIL

A wonderfully piquant and fragrant oil with a pronounced flavour of shallots and garlic. Add to salad dressings, or use to give a caramelized onion flavour to mashed potatoes.

Shelf-life: 6 months (sealed and refrigerated, the fried shallot mix can be stored for up to 1 month and used to top salads or to add texture to soups and stews)

| 150g (5oz) shallots, chopped |
| 10 garlic cloves, chopped |
| 5cm (2 inches) fresh ginger, shredded |
| 1–2 Thai chillies or fresh or dried bird's eye chillies, crushed |
| 1 litre (1¾ pints) oil |

Gently fry all the ingredients in the oil until the shallots are golden and just beginning to crisp, about 15–20 minutes. Remove from the heat and allow to cool. The oil is ready for use or can be filtered into a sterilized bottle (see pages 134–35).

LEMON OIL

| 1 litre (1¾ pints) oil |
| thinly grated zest of 5 lemons, all white pith removed |

Be sure to use unwaxed lemons for this oil.

Shelf-life: 6 months

Put the oil in a pan and warm to 60°C (140°F). Place the lemon zest in a sterilized jar or bottle (see pages 134–35), pour the oil in and seal. Keep the bottle in a warm place for about a week, shaking the bottle from time to time. Filter the oil into a sterilized bottle (see pages 134–35).

GARLIC OIL

| 4 heads of fresh garlic, cut across into halves |
| 4–5 sprigs of fresh thyme |
| 1 litre (1¾ pints) light olive oil |

The garlic may be roasted before being immersed in oil to give a nuttier, milder flavour. Simply place it in a roasting tin, sprinkle with a little oil and roast for 25–30 minutes, or until soft. The marinated garlic is wonderful in salsas and salads.

Shelf-life: 6 months

Place the garlic and thyme in a sterilized preserving jar (see pages 134–35), cover with the oil and seal tightly. Sterilize the sealed bottle and leave in a warm place for 2–3 weeks. The oil is then ready to use immediately, or it can be filtered and bottled for future use (see pages 134–35).

FRESH CHILLI OIL ▷

Hot, fragrant and wonderfully mellow, chilli oil can be used to dress pasta, salads or grilled fish or meat; I even use it as a barbecue baste. For decorative effect, add whole chillies to the oil after filtering – especially if offering this as a gift.

Shelf-life: 6 months

300g (10oz) red or green chillies, stalks removed, sliced in half

4–5 sprigs of fresh thyme

1 litre (1¾ pints) oil

1 Place the chillies, thyme and oil in a saucepan and bring to a simmer. Reduce the heat and allow to bubble gently for about 15 minutes.

2 Pour into a sterilized preserving jar (see pages 134–35), seal and leave to stand for 2 weeks to develop flavour. Filter and bottle the oil (see pages 134–35).

SMOKY CHILLI OIL

If you include bird's eye chillies this mild oil becomes a hot favourite for the chilli lover.

Shelf-life: 6 months

50g (1¾ oz) chipotle chillies, stalks removed, coarsely crushed

50g (1¾ oz) guindilla chillies, stalks removed, coarsely crushed

1 tbsp bird's eye chillies (optional), stalks removed, coarsely crushed

1 litre (1¾ pints) oil

Gently heat all the ingredients in a pan, but do not allow the oil to get hotter than 100°C (212°F). Simmer for 20 minutes, then remove from the heat and allow to cool. The oil is ready for use immediately or it can be filtered and bottled (see pages 134–35).

KAFFIR LIME OIL

A superbly fragrant and versatile oil. Use this to flavour vinaigrettes and mayonnaises and to drizzle over vegetable carpaccio or thinly sliced smoked meats and fish.

Shelf-life: 6 months

1 litre (1¾ pints) oil

thinly pared zest of 4 limes, all white pith removed

20 kaffir lime leaves

Warm the oil to 60°C (140°F), making sure that it does not get any hotter. Lightly bruise the zest and the leaves and put into a sterilized jar or bottle. Pour the warm oil over and seal. Leave in a cool, dark place for 2–3 weeks, then filter and bottle (see pages 134–35).

RIGHT: FRESH CHILLI OIL BEING POURED INTO A JAR

MAYONNAISE

The master recipe for making mayonnaise, including instructions for making it in a food processor, is on pages 38–39.

Shelf-life: *1 week in the refrigerator*

2 egg yolks, at cool room temperature
2 tsp lemon juice or white wine vinegar, plus a little extra to taste
1 tsp Dijon mustard or mustard powder
a small pinch of salt
300ml (½ pint) groundnut, light olive or light, flavourless oil such as sesame
salt and freshly ground black pepper

In a bowl, mix together the egg yolks, lemon juice or vinegar, mustard and salt. Whisking continuously, start adding the oil a drop at a time until about one third has been amalgamated. Continuing to whisk, pour in the rest of the oil in a thin, steady stream until the mayonnaise is thick and glossy. Whisk in lemon juice or vinegar and salt and freshly ground black pepper to taste.

VARIATIONS

GARLIC MAYONNAISE
This is delicious as a dip or served with fish, cold chicken or steamed vegetables. Follow the recipe above, using lemon juice rather than vinegar. Mash 4–6 garlic cloves to a paste with a little salt and mix this into the finished mayonnaise along with 2 tablespoons chopped fresh herbs, such as thyme, oregano, mint, parsley, dill or marjoram. Season with salt and freshly ground pepper.

HERB MAYONNAISE
Serve this with fish or as a salad dressing. Stir 3 tablespoons Herb Purée (see page 42) and 1 tablespoon lemon juice into the finished mayonnaise. Season to taste.

SMOKY RED PEPPER MAYONNAISE
Roast, peel and purée 2 red peppers (see page 96), then place in a muslin-lined sieve and drain for 2 hours. Stir the drained purée and 2 tablespoons lemon juice into the finished mayonnaise. Season with salt and black pepper.

ORANGE MUSTARD MAYONNAISE
This is delicious with poached fish, especially salmon. Bring the juice of 3 oranges to the boil in a small pan and simmer for 15–20 minutes, until reduced by three quarters. Remove from the heat and allow to cool, then mix into the finished mayonnaise along with the grated zest of 1 orange, 1 tablespoon lemon juice and 3–4 tablespoons grainy mustard such as *moutarde de meaux*. Season to taste with salt and freshly ground black pepper.

BEETROOT MAYONNAISE
Purée 100g (3½oz) cooked beetroot and 2 tablespoons red or white wine vinegar in a food processor. Pass the purée through a sieve, then stir it into the finished mayonnaise and season with salt and freshly ground black pepper.

HARISSA MAYONNAISE
For a chilli-spiked mayonnaise, stir 3–4 tablespoons Harissa (see page 103) into the finished mayonnaise.

PRAWN COCKTAIL SAUCE
Make this classic sauce by stirring 4 tablespoons tomato ketchup, 1 tablespoon Worcestershire sauce, 1 tablespoon lemon juice and Tabasco or cayenne pepper to taste into the finished mayonnaise. Season with salt and freshly ground pepper.

GREEN GODDESS DRESSING *See page 11 for illustration*
This classic American sauce, created in the 1920s by the chef at San Francisco's Palace Hotel, is wonderful served with steak or grilled fish. Stir 100ml (3½fl oz) soured cream, 4 finely chopped spring onions, 4 finely chopped anchovy fillets, 3 tablespoons finely chopped fresh parsley and 2 tablespoons tarragon vinegar into the finished mayonnaise. Season to taste with salt and freshly ground black pepper.

HERB MAYONNAISE

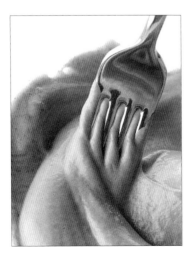

SMOKY RED PEPPER MAYONNAISE

ORANGE MUSTARD MAYONNAISE

BEETROOT MAYONNAISE

GRIBICHE

A delicious version of mayonnaise that goes well with fish or hard-boiled eggs; it also makes a very good dip for raw or steamed vegetables.

Shelf-life: 1 week in the refrigerator

3 hard-boiled egg yolks
1 raw egg yolk
1 tbsp Dijon mustard
250ml (8fl oz) olive oil
1 tbsp white wine vinegar
3 hard-boiled egg whites, chopped or coarsely grated
2 tbsp capers, chopped
2 tbsp cornichons or sour gherkins, chopped
2 tbsp chopped fresh *fines herbes* (chervil, chives, parsley, tarragon)
salt and freshly ground black pepper

Either push the hard-boiled egg yolks through a sieve into a bowl or mash with a fork. Add the raw egg yolk and mustard and mix to make a smooth paste. Start adding the oil in a trickle, whisking continuously, until half the oil has been added. Mix in the vinegar and, still whisking, slowly add the rest of the oil. The sauce should be thick and shiny. Add the rest of the ingredients and mix well.

VARIATION

TARTARE SAUCE
Follow the recipe above but omit the egg whites and the cornichons or gherkins. Increase the quantity of capers to 3 tablespoons, add 60g (2oz) finely chopped onion or shallots and use finely chopped parsley instead of the *fines herbes*.

AÏOLI

4–6 garlic cloves, any green sprouts removed
¼ tsp salt
2 hard-boiled egg yolks, rubbed through a fine sieve
1 raw egg yolk
300ml (½ pint) olive oil
lemon juice

Put the garlic and salt in a food processor and whizz to a smooth paste. Add the boiled and raw egg yolks and process to mix. With the machine running, start adding the oil a drop at a time, then in a thin, steady stream. Finish by adding lemon juice to taste, pulsing briefly to mix.

A classic French sauce so called because of the large quantity of garlic (ail) that is used to make it. Some recipes recommend using up to 2 garlic cloves per person, which produces a highly flavoured, pungent sauce.

Shelf-life: 1 week in the refrigerator

RÉMOULADE

1 quantity of Mayonnaise (see opposite)
1 tbsp finely chopped gherkin
1 tbsp finely chopped capers
1 tbsp each chopped fresh parsley, chervil and tarragon
1 tbsp Dijon mustard
3–4 anchovy fillets, finely chopped

Mix all the ingredients together in a bowl.

Serve this with fish or cold meats or as a dip for steamed vegetables.

Advance preparation: the mayonnaise can be made in advance

Shelf-life: 1 week in the refrigerator

YOGURTTAISE

A lighter and much less calorific version of traditional mayonnaise. For extra body and a creamier texture, drain the yogurt and fromage frais beforehand: pour each one into a separate cheesecloth-lined sieve over a bowl and leave to drain in the refrigerator for 5–6 hours.

200ml (7fl oz) Greek-style yogurt, well chilled
200ml (7fl oz) fromage frais, well chilled
1 tbsp Dijon or English mustard
strained juice of 1 lemon
grated zest of ½ lemon (optional)
75ml (2½fl oz) olive, groundnut or hazelnut oil
salt and freshly ground black pepper

BY HAND: combine the yogurt, fromage frais, mustard, lemon juice and zest, if using, in a bowl. Whisk in a few drops of the oil. Pour in a little more oil and, continuing to whisk, gradually add the rest of it until the mixture is glossy and thickly coats the back of a spoon. Season to taste with salt and black pepper.

MACHINE METHOD: put all the ingredients except the oil in a food processor. With the machine on high speed, slowly add the oil in a thin, steady stream.

Shelf-life: 1 week in the refrigerator

FLAVOURED BUTTERS

THESE BUTTERS ARE A FAST AND INNOVATIVE way of adding instant flavour to a whole host of dishes. Spread over bread, they transform canapés and sandwiches, while stirred into sauces and stews in the final cooking stages they enhance the texture and flavour. The butters can be served with roast meats, chicken or fish; melted, they make wonderful dipping sauces for prawns or steamed vegetables, for example.

Traditionally the ingredients are pounded in a pestle and mortar, but they are much easier to mix in a food processor or blender. I like a textured butter but for smoother results, rub the butter through a drum sieve with the help of a plastic scraper. Flavoured butters are best eaten fresh, but tightly wrapped they do keep well and, for convenience, I always have one or two varieties in my refrigerator or freezer.

CHILLI BUTTER

This is especially good with barbecued or grilled fish and chicken.

Shelf-life: *1 week in the refrigerator; 1 month in the freezer*

1 red pepper, roasted, peeled and deseeded (see page 96)
200g (7oz) unsalted butter, softened
1 tbsp lemon juice
1–2 red or green chillies or a mixture, deseeded and very finely chopped
1 tbsp finely chopped fresh coriander (optional)
salt

1 Purée the pepper in a blender or food processor. Pour the purée into a muslin-lined sieve over a bowl and set aside to drain for 1 hour.

2 Place the butter in a bowl, add the drained pepper purée and the lemon juice and beat until light and fluffy. Mix in the chilli and the coriander, if using, and add salt to taste. Roll (see below) and chill until firm.

ROLLING BUTTER

1 Divide the butter into halves and place on a piece of greaseproof paper, foil or clingfilm.

2 Roll each one into an even sausage shape and secure by twisting the ends.

LEMONGRASS & LIME BUTTER

250g (8oz) unsalted butter, softened
4 lemongrass stalks, hard outer layers removed, finely chopped or pounded
2 tbsp lime juice
salt
1 small chilli, deseeded and finely chopped (optional)
5 kaffir lime leaves, finely shredded

An exceptionally fresh and fragrant butter that will add a wonderful aromatic tanginess to seafood or fish; it can also be spread on bread or used in canapés.

Shelf-life: *1 week in the refrigerator; 1 month in the freezer*

1 Heat 100g (3½oz) of the butter in a small pan, add the lemongrass and fry gently until it begins to colour. Remove from the heat and set aside to cool, then strain through a muslin-lined sieve.

2 In a bowl, beat the remaining butter until light and fluffy. Add the strained butter and the rest of the ingredients and mix well. Roll (see left) and chill until firm.

TOMATO BUTTER

100g (3½oz) sun-dried tomatoes in oil, well drained
200g (7oz) unsalted butter, softened
2 tbsp shredded fresh basil
salt and freshly ground black pepper

This is delicious on canapés or on bread. For a more textured butter, purée half the tomatoes and coarsely chop the rest by hand before adding to the butter.

Shelf-life: *1 week in the refrigerator; 1 month in the freezer*

Purée the tomatoes in a food processor or blender, then add the butter and blend well. Add the basil and season with salt, if necessary, and pepper. Roll (see left) and chill until firm.

ANCHOVY BUTTER

A classic accompaniment to poached or grilled fish, this wonderfully flavoured butter is surprisingly good with juicy grilled steak.

Shelf-life: 1 week in the refrigerator; 1 month in the freezer

100g (3½oz) anchovy fillets, salted or in oil, soaked in cold water for a few minutes

200g (7oz) unsalted butter, softened

2–3 tbsp chopped fresh basil or dill

1–2 tbsp lemon juice (optional)

salt, if necessary, and freshly ground black pepper

Either pound the anchovies in a pestle and mortar or purée in a food processor. Add the butter and blend well. Add the basil or dill, the lemon juice, if using, and season to taste. Roll into a sausage shape (see opposite) and chill until firm.

LEMON BUTTER

This is delicious with smoked salmon sandwiches, grilled fish or to add a subtle lemon flavour to sauces. For lime butter use lime juice and zest instead of lemon.

Shelf-life: 1 week in the refrigerator; 1 month in the freezer

200g (7oz) unsalted butter, softened

4 tbsp lemon juice

grated zest of 1 lemon

1–2 tbsp chopped fresh dill or parsley (optional)

salt and freshly ground black pepper

Place the butter in a bowl and beat with the lemon juice until light and fluffy. Add the rest of the ingredients and mix well. Roll (see opposite) and chill until firm.

GARLIC BUTTER

One of the essential stand-bys of my kitchen; spread it thickly on a baguette for the classic garlic bread, or add to hot stews or soups for a subtle aroma of freshly mashed garlic.

Shelf-life: 1 week in the refrigerator; 1 month in the freezer

200g (7oz) unsalted butter, softened

1 tbsp lemon juice (optional)

4–6 garlic cloves, puréed

2 tbsp finely chopped fresh parsley (optional)

salt and freshly ground black pepper

Place the butter in a bowl and beat with the lemon juice until light and fluffy. Add the garlic and parsley, if using, season to taste and mix well. Roll into a sausage shape (see opposite) and chill until firm.

RIGHT, FROM TOP TO BOTTOM: ANCHOVY, CHILLI, LEMONGRASS & LIME, TOMATO AND GARLIC BUTTERS

COOKING SAUCES

IT IS HARD TO DEFINE COOKING SAUCES AND YET EVERY CUISINE HAS THEM — BASIC SAUCE-LIKE STEWS TO

WHICH MEAT, FISH OR VEGETABLES ARE ADDED AND COOKED AND THE FLAVOURS INFUSED. THESE HEARTY

SAUCES CAN BE STRETCHED TO FEED LARGE NUMBERS IF NECESSARY; THEY ARE DESIGNED TO BE EATEN WITH

BREAD, NOODLES, RICE OR OTHER STARCHY ACCOMPANIMENTS FOR A SATISFYING MEAL.

SPICY TOMATO & CHILLI SAUCE FOR FISH ▷

This hot, piquant sauce is ideal as a base for fish stew. It can also be poured, hot or cold, over fried, grilled or poached fish.

Enough for 1kg (2lb) fish fillets or steaks

Shelf-life: *3 weeks in the refrigerator*

See page 15 for illustration

4 tbsp olive oil

2 onions, chopped

6 garlic cloves, chopped

6 anchovy fillets

750g (1½lb) plum tomatoes, quartered

1 tart apple, peeled, cored and chopped

2–3 tbsp tomato purée (optional)

juice and grated zest of 1 lemon

2–3 red chillies (or more to taste), such as red jalapeño, Anaheim or serrano, finely chopped

salt, if necessary

1 Heat the oil in a pan, add the onions, garlic and anchovies and fry until the onions are translucent and soft.

2 Add the tomatoes and apple and simmer for about 30 minutes or until most of the liquid has evaporated.

3 Transfer to a food processor and process to a smooth sauce.

4 Pass through a sieve into a clean pan, then add the tomato purée, if using, lemon juice and zest and the chillies. Bring to the boil and boil for 2–3 minutes. Add salt if necessary (the anchovies are salty).

5 To use: either pour over fish steaks and bake for about 25 minutes or simply serve as an accompaniment to poached, grilled or fried fish.

VARIATIONS

SPICY TOMATO & FENNEL SAUCE
Fry finely chopped celery heart, 1 finely chopped small fennel bulb and ½ teaspoon fennel seeds with the onion, garlic and anchovies in step 1.

SPICY PEPPER SAUCE
Substitute 1kg (2lb) deseeded and sliced red peppers for the tomatoes. Omit the apple and the tomato purée.

OPPOSITE: COD FILLETS IN SPICY TOMATO & CHILLI SAUCE

DRY CURRY

Dry curries vary in strength and flavour but all are based on a flavouring paste which is fried with the meat until it browns, then a little liquid is added and the meat is cooked until tender. This recipe is especially good made with lamb, beef or mutton but also works well with vegetables. For an authentic flavour, use a stone grinder to make the spice paste, and relish its full aroma. The masala (a spice mix, usually dry-roasted whole, then ground) is also integral to the curry's distinctive flavours.

For the spice paste

3 onions, chopped

6 garlic cloves, peeled

5cm (2 inches) fresh ginger, peeled

2–6 thin green chillies (to taste), deseeded

1 tsp turmeric

1 tsp chilli powder

For the masala

6 green cardamom pods

6 cloves

2 tsp coriander seeds

1 tsp cumin seeds

5cm (2 inches) cinnamon stick or a few pieces of cassia

For the curry

4 tbsp ghee or oil

750g (1½lb) stewing lamb, beef or mutton, cubed

3 tbsp yogurt, beaten with 250ml (8fl oz) water

8 fresh curry leaves (optional)

chopped fresh coriander, to serve

1 To make the spice paste, put all the ingredients in a food processor and process to a smooth purée.

2 Make the masala as shown below.

3 Heat the ghee or oil in a large pan, add the spice paste and fry for 2–3 minutes or until it begins to give off a pleasant aroma. Add the meat, sprinkle with half the masala and fry, stirring and scraping the base of the pan, for 15–20 minutes or until nicely browned.

4 Reduce the heat, sprinkle with about 3 tablespoons of the diluted yogurt, then cover and simmer very slowly for about 1½–2 hours, adding more yogurt when the mixture becomes dry. If all the yogurt has been used and the meat is still not tender, add a little water as necessary.

5 Five minutes before the meat is ready, stir in the remaining masala and the curry leaves, if using. Sprinkle with coriander and serve with rice.

Advance preparation: the masala can be stored in an airtight container for up to 3 months; the spice paste keeps for 1 week in the refrigerator and 3 months in the freezer

Shelf-life: 1 week in the refrigerator; 3 months in the freezer

DRY-ROASTING SPICES & MAKING MASALA

1 To dry-roast spices, fry them in a dry frying pan over a medium heat until they are lightly browned and beginning to give off an appetizing spicy aroma. Be careful not to burn them – they are ready when they start to pop.

2 If you are making a masala or spice mix, set the roasted spices aside to cool, then transfer to a spice or coffee mill or a mortar.

3 Process in the spice or coffee mill or pound to a fine powder with a pestle and mortar.

4 For a finer powder, sieve the powder and grind the larger pieces left in the sieve again.

DRY VEGETABLE CURRY

This is a modern adaptation of an Indian classic. Traditionally cauliflower or cabbage are used but I prefer a mixture of vegetables such as green beans, baby carrots, small tender squashes and, best of all, pumpkin or sweet potato. You can make this recipe with paneer or tofu but fry it gently in oil until lightly browned before adding it to the stew.

Advance preparation: the masala can be stored in an airtight container for up to 3 months; the spice paste keeps for 1 week in the refrigerator and 3 months in the freezer

Shelf-life: 1 week in the refrigerator; 3 months in the freezer

For the masala

1 tsp coriander seeds

4 black or green cardamom pods

5cm (2 inches) cinnamon stick or 2–3 pieces of cassia

$\frac{1}{2}$ tsp fennel seeds

2 tsp nigella seeds

For the curry

4 tbsp ghee or oil

1 tbsp mixed black and white mustard seeds

2 tbsp white poppy seeds

1 quantity of Spice Paste (see Dry Curry, opposite)

4 tbsp yogurt, beaten with 200ml (7fl oz) water

500g (1lb) mixed vegetables, such as cauliflower, potato, peas and green beans, steamed, blanched or fried in oil

chopped fresh coriander, to serve

1 For the masala, dry-roast all the spices except the nigella seeds, then grind them (see opposite). Dry-roast the nigella seeds and stir them into the masala.

2 Heat the ghee or oil in a large pan, add the black and white mustard seeds and the poppy seeds and fry for 1–2 minutes, until they start to pop. Add the spice paste and fry for 2–3 minutes or until it gives off a pleasant aroma. Sprinkle with half the masala and fry for 15–20 minutes or until nicely browned.

3 Reduce the heat, sprinkle with about half the diluted yogurt, then cover and simmer very slowly for about 20 minutes, adding more yogurt when the mixture becomes too dry.

4 Add the vegetables, turning them well in the sauce, then add the rest of the yogurt and heat through. Stir in the rest of the masala. Sprinkle with coriander and serve with rice.

ANGLO-INDIAN CURRY

3 tbsp ghee or oil

500g (1lb) onions, chopped

2 garlic cloves, chopped (optional)

2 large dessert apples, peeled, cored and chopped

1–2 tbsp mild curry powder (to taste)

2 bay leaves, crumbled

a small piece of cinnamon stick or cassia

100g (3$\frac{1}{2}$oz) sultanas or raisins, plumped up in a little hot water

500ml (17fl oz) Chicken or Vegetable Stock (see pages 28 and 31) or water

salt

1 Heat the ghee or oil in a large pan, add the onions and the garlic, if using, and fry until golden. Stir in the apples, curry powder, bay leaves and cinnamon or cassia and cook over a high heat, stirring constantly, for about 3 minutes.

2 Add the sultanas or raisins and the stock or water. Bring to the boil, then reduce the heat and simmer for about 30 minutes or until most of the liquid has evaporated and the sauce has thickened. Season with salt to taste.

3 To use: either add cooked meat or vegetables and heat through thoroughly, or pour over hot cooked meat.

This pleasant, mild and versatile curry was invented in the kitchens of colonial India, where local cooks adapted traditional curries to suit the British palate. This sauce became very popular in Victorian Britain as a way of using up yesterday's roast, but you can also fry meat until lightly browned, then heat it in the sauce until cooked through.

Enough for 500–750g (1–1$\frac{1}{2}$lb) meat or vegetables

Advance preparation: the stock can be made in advance

Shelf-life: 1 week in the refrigerator; 3 months in the freezer

LAMB KORMA ▷

Korma is a technique rather than a sauce, by which meat or vegetables are braised in a sauce thickened with onions, yogurt, ground nuts and aromatics. After long, slow cooking, the dish is finished with more yogurt or cream. The superbly intricate flavour of the korma is achieved by the order and timing in which the spices and aromatics are added to the sauce. Here is a modern version of this north Indian dish.

Advance preparation: the masala can be stored in an airtight container for up to 3 months; the spice paste keeps for 1 week in the refrigerator and 3 months in the freezer

Shelf-life: 1 week in the refrigerator; 3 months in the freezer

For the spice paste

4 onions, chopped

4 garlic cloves, peeled

5cm (2 inches) fresh ginger, peeled

3–4 red chillies, deseeded

60g (2oz) almonds or cashew nuts, ground

For the masala

6 green cardamom pods

5–6 cloves

2.5cm (1 inch) cinnamon stick

1 tsp coriander seeds

2 bay leaves

For the stew

6 tbsp ghee or oil

750g (1½lb) lean lamb, mutton or beef

1 tbsp white poppy seeds, ground (optional)

200ml (7fl oz) yogurt, beaten with 150ml (¼ pint) water

5 tbsp double cream or thick yogurt

12 slivered almonds, browned in the oven or in a little oil

2–3 tbsp fresh mint or coriander leaves

1 To make the spice paste, process all the ingredients together in a food processor until as smooth as possible.

2 Make the masala (see page 78).

3 Heat the ghee or oil in a large pan, add the spice paste and fry for 5–8 minutes or until it gives off a pleasant, spicy aroma. Add the meat and sprinkle with the poppy seeds, if using, and three quarters of the masala, mixing all well in.

4 Fry, stirring frequently and scraping the base of the pan, for about 10–15 minutes or until the mixture dries and starts to brown. Reduce the heat, then add 3 tablespoons of the diluted yogurt, cover and cook gently for 20–25 minutes, stirring and scraping frequently. Add more of the diluted yogurt as necessary to prevent sticking.

5 Stir in the rest of the diluted yogurt, bring to the boil, then reduce the heat and simmer for about 1–1½ hours or until the meat is tender and the sauce has reduced and thickened. Skim off any traces of fat floating on the surface. Add the rest of the masala and the cream or yogurt and boil rapidly for 2 minutes, until the sauce is smooth.

6 Sprinkle with the almonds and mint or coriander and serve.

VARIATIONS

CHICKEN KORMA

Make a masala with 2 teaspoons coriander seeds, 1 teaspoon cumin seeds, 2.5cm (1 inch) cinnamon stick or cassia, 1 teaspoon fennel seeds, ½ teaspoon mace and 1 teaspoon sweet or hot paprika, then follow the recipe above, replacing the lamb, mutton or beef with 4–6 skinless chicken portions. Dissolve ¼ teaspoon saffron in a few tablespoons of warm milk or water and add with the chicken.

PANEER OR TOFU KORMA

Korma can easily be adapted for vegetarians. Simply replace the meat with 750g (1½lb) paneer or tofu, drained on kitchen paper and cut into cubes.
• Fry the paneer or tofu in 3 tablespoons of the ghee or oil in a pan until golden on all sides. Lift out on to kitchen paper and set aside.
• Add the rest of the oil, the spice paste, poppy seeds and three quarters of the masala and fry until the spice paste starts to brown. Stir in 4–5 tablespoons of the diluted yogurt and bring to the boil. Reduce the heat and simmer for 10 minutes, stirring and scraping the bottom of the pan, then add the rest of the yogurt mix and bring to the boil. Lower the heat and simmer for about 25 minutes, uncovered, until the sauce has reduced and thickened.
• Add the paneer or tofu, the double cream or yogurt and the rest of the masala and simmer for 5–8 minutes until heated through. Sprinkle with the almonds and herbs before serving.

ROGAN JOSH

Josh are a vast family of juicy curries in which the aromatics are not pulverized into a paste but used whole. A little masala is added towards the end of cooking for a fresher flavour. Serve this delicious dish with cinnamon-flavoured rice or, as I like to eat it, with warm naan or pitta bread.

Advance preparation:
the masala can be stored in an airtight container for up to 3 months; the fried spice paste keeps for 1 week in the refrigerator and 3 months in the freezer

Shelf-life: 1 week in the refrigerator; 3 months in the freezer

3 tbsp oil or ghee
6 cloves
5cm (2 inch) cinnamon stick, broken, or 2 pieces of cassia
2–4 small dried red chillies, such as bird's eye, deseeded and chopped
2 bay leaves, crumbled
3 onions, grated or finely chopped
4 garlic cloves, crushed
2.5cm (1 inch) fresh ginger, finely shredded
500g (1lb) lamb, beef or mutton, cut into 2.5cm (1 inch) cubes
4 tbsp yogurt, mixed with 300ml (½ pint) water or stock
1–2 tsp masala (see Lamb Korma, page 80)
2–3 tbsp chopped fresh coriander

1 Heat the oil or ghee in a large pan, add the cloves and fry for 2 minutes. Stir in the cinnamon or cassia, chillies and bay leaves and fry for 2–3 minutes or until the bay starts to colour. Add the onions, garlic and ginger and cook for 15–20 minutes or until the onions are golden brown.

2 Add the meat and fry for about 15 minutes or until nicely brown. If the mixture gets too dry, add a few tablespoons of the diluted yogurt.

3 Add the remaining yogurt, bring to the boil, then reduce the heat and simmer very slowly for about 1–1½ hours or until the meat is tender and the sauce has reduced and thickened. Skim any traces of fat from the surface, then stir in the masala and coriander and serve.

VARIATIONS

TOMATO JOSH
Replace the yogurt with 375g (12oz) tomatoes, peeled, deseeded (see page 43) and chopped, and 2 tablespoons tomato purée.

METHI JOSH
Add 150g (5oz) very finely chopped fresh fenugreek with the onions, garlic and ginger in step 1.

VANILLA CURRY

For the spice paste
1 large onion, chopped
3 garlic cloves, peeled
2.5cm (1 inch) fresh ginger, peeled
2–3 long, thin red chillies, deseeded
For the stew
3 tbsp oil or ghee
1 vanilla pod, finely chopped
4 tbsp yogurt, mixed with 300ml (½ pint) coconut milk or water
1 medium pineapple, peeled, cored and finely chopped
3–4 tbsp chopped fresh coriander or dill
salt

1 To make the spice paste, put all the ingredients in a food processor and process to a smooth purée.

2 Heat the oil or ghee in a large pan, add half the vanilla and fry for 1–2 minutes or until it starts to give off a pleasant aroma. Add the spice paste and fry for about 10 minutes, stirring and scraping the base of the pan, until evenly golden brown. If the mixture is too dry, add a spoonful or two of the yogurt mixture.

3 Add the pineapple and fry for about 5 minutes or until it starts to soften. Add the yogurt mixture, bring to the boil, then reduce the heat and simmer very slowly for about 45 minutes, until the sauce has reduced and thickened. Stir in the coriander or dill and season with salt to taste.

4 To use: pour the sauce over browned duck or chicken pieces and simmer for 1–1½ hours, or until the meat is tender. Alternatively, the sauce can be poured over grilled or barbecued poultry.

This is probably my favourite recipe in the book – it is delicately flavoured, well balanced and has a delightfully subtle aroma of vanilla. It is superb with duck and also goes well with free-range chicken or game birds. Since I created this curry I have experimented and made it with peach and mango instead of pineapple – both with excellent results. For a stronger vanilla flavour, I sometimes sprinkle the dish with a little finely chopped vanilla pod just before serving.

Enough for about 500–750g (1–1½ lb) duck or chicken

Advance preparation:
the fried spice paste (without the coconut milk) keeps for 2 weeks in the refrigerator and 3 months in the freezer

Shelf-life: 1 week in the refrigerator; 3 months in the freezer

SABZI

In Iran brides were judged on their ability to prepare this superbly delicate and herby dish. Minutely chopping the enormous quantity of herbs required a great deal of skill – rendered particularly arduous under the watchful eye of the mother-in-law. These days the herbs are chopped in a food processor or in a specially designed mill. Dried limes, or lamoo, are a popular flavouring in Iranian food and are available in Middle Eastern and Indian shops – if you can't find them, omit them altogether. Serve with plain boiled rice, or a rice or burghul pilaff.

Advance preparation: the fried herb mixture keeps for 2 weeks in the refrigerator and 3 months in the freezer

Shelf-life: 1 week in the refrigerator; 3 months in the freezer

250g (8oz) leeks

100g (3½oz) fresh flat-leaf parsley (leaves only)

100g (3½oz) fresh coriander (leaves and stalks)

100g (3½oz) green garlic or garlic chives (optional)

100g (3½oz) fresh dill, hard stems removed

100g (3½oz) fresh mint (leaves only)

50g (1¼oz) fresh fenugreek, hard stems removed

125ml (4fl oz) sesame or olive oil

100g (3½oz) dried kidney beans, soaked in cold water overnight, then drained

3 onions, chopped

750g (1½lb) shoulder or leg of lamb, cut into large chunks

Chicken Stock (see page 28) or water to cover

4 dried limes, rinsed in boiling water and pierced in several places with the point of a sharp knife

2 tbsp lime juice

salt

1 Wash and dry the leeks and herbs, then chop very finely by hand or in a food processor. Heat about three quarters of the oil in a large, heavy-based frying pan and add the leeks and herbs. Fry over a medium heat, turning the mixture constantly, for 20–25 minutes or until it darkens. If too dry, add a little water to help keep it moving. Put the kidney beans in a separate pan, cover with water, then boil hard for 10 minutes. Drain well.

2 Heat the remaining oil in a deep pan and fry the onions until soft and golden. Add the meat and fry until browned. Add the herb mixture, the beans and enough stock or water to cover. Bring to the boil, then reduce the heat, cover and simmer gently for 45 minutes.

3 Add the limes and some salt and simmer for 45–60 minutes or until the meat is tender and the sauce has thickened. Stir in the lime juice and season with salt.

PLUM SAUCE FOR FISH

3 tbsp sesame or groundnut oil

a small piece of cinnamon, crumbled

1–2 dried bird's eye chillies

100g (3½oz) red or ordinary shallots, chopped

5 garlic cloves, chopped

2.5cm (1 inch) fresh ginger, finely chopped or grated

300g (10oz) Victoria or Switzen plums, stoned and coarsely chopped

300ml (½ pint) Fish Stock (see page 30), rice wine or dry white wine

1 tbsp dark soy sauce

1–1½ tbsp sugar

2 star anise

½ tsp ground Szechuan pepper

salt

1 Heat the oil in a wok or a large frying pan, add the cinnamon and chillies and fry over a high heat for 2–3 minutes or until the cinnamon gives off a pleasant aroma and the chillies are browned. Lift out and discard. Add the shallots, garlic and ginger and fry for 5 minutes or until the shallots soften and start to colour.

2 Add all the remaining ingredients and bring to the boil. Reduce the heat and simmer for about 30 minutes or until the sauce has thickened and reduced.

3 Either use the sauce as it is or purée in a blender and sieve for a smooth texture.

4 To use: either pour over raw fish and bake until the fish is done, or bring to the boil and pour over baked or steamed fish, allow the fish to absorb the flavour for a few minutes, then serve.

A fragrant, delicate sauce that goes well with freshwater fish such as carp, trout or tilapia but is also delicious with oily seafish such as mackerel or sardines.

Enough for 500g (1lb) fish

Advance preparation: the fish stock can be made in advance

Shelf-life: 1 week in the refrigerator; 3 months in the freezer

SWEET & SOUR SAUCE

This sauce is rumoured to have been invented by Chinese cooks in the railroad canteens of the Wild West. It became one of the most used and abused of Chinese sauces. Made properly, sweet and sour sauce is delicious and versatile – serve it with chicken, fish or pork, or as a dip or side sauce.

Enough for 750g (1½lb) chicken, fish or pork

Shelf-life: 2 weeks in the refrigerator; 3 months in the freezer

3 tbsp groundnut or sesame oil, or lard
4 garlic cloves, finely shredded
2.5cm (1 inch) fresh ginger, finely shredded
1 carrot, finely shredded
1–2 hot red chillies such as Thai or bird's eye, deseeded and shredded (optional)
150ml (¼ pint) water
150ml (¼ pint) rice vinegar
150ml (¼ pint) tomato ketchup
4–5 tbsp good honey or sugar
1–2 tbsp cornflour, potato flour or arrowroot, dissolved in 2 tbsp water

1 Heat the oil or lard in a wok or a large frying pan, add the garlic, ginger, carrot and chillies, if using, and fry for a few minutes until softened. Add all the remaining ingredients except the cornflour, potato flour or arrowroot. Bring to the boil, then reduce the heat and simmer for 5 minutes.

2 Add the cornflour, potato flour or arrowroot and simmer for a few minutes or until the sauce has thickened.

3 To use: bring to the boil, pour over hot fried or grilled food and serve immediately.

VARIATION

FRUITY SWEET & SOUR SAUCE
Replace the water with pineapple, peach, passion fruit or apricot juice and add about 75g (2½oz) of the corresponding finely chopped fresh fruit in the final stages of cooking. Omit the honey or sugar. You could also use tinned fruit and a little of the syrup to taste.

BLACK BEAN SAUCE

4 tbsp groundnut or sesame oil
2 garlic cloves, finely chopped
1cm (½ inch) fresh ginger, shredded
1–2 red or green chillies, deseeded and chopped
3 tbsp salted black beans, soaked in cold water for 20 minutes, then drained and coarsely chopped
1 tsp rice flour or cornflour
350ml (12fl oz) Chicken Stock (see page 28)
1 tbsp sweet soy sauce or 1 tbsp dark soy sauce and 2 tsp dark brown sugar
2 tbsp rice wine or sherry
1–2 tsp dark sesame oil

You either like or dislike the flavour of fermented and salted black beans. Here they are used to make one of China's most classic sauces. I also use them instead of salt in meat and vegetable stews. Salted black beans can be bought in any Chinese food shop.

Enough for 500g (1lb) chicken, lamb, beef or seafood and 1kg (2lb) mussels

Shelf-life: 2 weeks in the refrigerator; 3 months in the freezer

1 Heat the oil in a wok or a large frying pan. Add the garlic, ginger and chillies and stir-fry for 1 minute. Add the black beans and stir-fry for 1–2 minutes or until the garlic starts to change colour.

2 Dissolve the rice flour or cornflour in a tablespoon of the chicken stock and add to the pan with the remaining stock and all the rest of the ingredients. Bring to the boil, stirring constantly, and cook for 1–2 minutes or until thickened.

3 To use: add to beef, lamb, chicken or fish in the final stages of stir-frying, or use to steam mussels and other seafood.

RED CURRY PASTE

A wonderful hot, sweet and fragrant adaptation of a Southeast Asian classic. Other fruit, such as papaya, mango or banana, can be substituted for the pineapple.

Enough for about 500–750g (1–1½lb) fish or meat

Shelf-life: 1 week in the refrigerator; 6 months in sealed jars (see pages 134–35)

1 large onion, coarsely chopped

6 garlic cloves, peeled

1 small pineapple, peeled, cored and coarsely chopped

4–6 large red chillies (to taste)

5cm (2 inches) fresh ginger or galangal, coarsely chopped

6 tbsp groundnut or sesame oil

2 tbsp sugar

3 tbsp Thai fish sauce (*nam pla*)

100ml (3½fl oz) coconut milk

1 Place the onion, garlic, pineapple, chillies and ginger or galangal in a baking tin, sprinkle with the oil and sugar and mix well. Place in an oven preheated to 190°C/375°F/Gas Mark 5 and bake, turning the ingredients and basting with the pan juices occasionally, for about 1 hour or until evenly browned.

2 Allow to cool slightly, then process to a smooth purée in a food processor or blender. Transfer the purée to a clean pan, add the fish sauce and coconut milk, then bring to the boil and cook, stirring constantly, for 3–4 minutes or until the sauce has thickened and most of the liquid has evaporated.

3 To use: put 4–6 tablespoons of the paste and 400ml (14fl oz) coconut milk in a pan with meat or fish that has been cut into cubes and simmer until cooked. The paste can also be rubbed on raw meat and left to marinate for 2–3 hours before roasting.

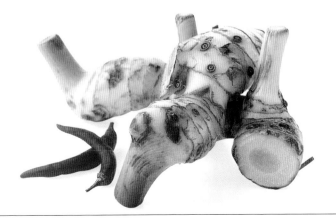

YELLOW CURRY PASTE

For the spice paste

150g (5oz) red shallots or onions, chopped

4 garlic cloves, peeled

3 lemongrass stalks, hard outer layers removed, chopped

1–3 yellow or green chillies (to taste), such as green bird's eye, deseeded

1cm (½ inch) fresh galangal or ginger

3 tbsp Thai fish sauce (*nam pla*)

For the curry

4 tbsp sesame or groundnut oil

½ tsp turmeric

4 tbsp yellow bean paste

75g (2½oz) tamarind pulp, soaked in 200ml (7fl oz) hot water, then sieved (see page 124)

1 tsp palm sugar or soft brown sugar

400ml (14fl oz) coconut milk

100ml (3½fl oz) water

5 tbsp chopped basil

1 For the spice paste, place all the ingredients in a blender or food processor and process to a smooth purée. If too dry add 1–2 tablespoons of water.

2 Heat the oil in a wok or frying pan, add the turmeric and fry for 1 minute. Add the spice paste and fry for 8–10 minutes, until it is fragrant and starting to brown.

3 Add the yellow bean paste, tamarind water and sugar and mix well, mashing and mixing the paste into the liquid. Bring to the boil, then reduce the heat and simmer for 15 minutes or until thickened. Add the coconut milk and water and boil for 2–3 minutes.

4 To use: pour over fish steaks that have been dusted with cornflour and lightly fried in oil. Simmer for 8–10 minutes, until the fish is done, then serve sprinkled with the chopped basil.

Yellow bean paste is rather an acquired taste. Strongly aromatic, it is made from unsalted, fermented soy beans. Like Japanese miso, it is used to flavour and thicken sauces, stews and soups. Yellow bean paste is available in jars or tins at most Chinese and Southeast Asian food shops.

Enough for about 500–750g (1–1½lb) fish

Advance preparation: the fried spice paste keeps for 1 week in the refrigerator and 3 months in the freezer

Shelf-life: 1 week in the refrigerator; 3 months in the freezer

LIGHT CURRY FOR FISH

Here is a Thai-style curry that is best served over rice noodles. It is delicious with any firm-fleshed fish, cut into cubes, or a combination of seafood such as prawns and scallops. You can also cook steamed vegetables, tofu or paneer in this sauce. If using tofu or paneer, brown it first in a little oil before adding it to the curry in the final cooking stages.

Enough for 500–750g (1–1½lb) fish

Advance preparation: the fried spice paste (without the coconut milk) keeps for 2 weeks in the refrigerator and 3 months in the freezer

Shelf-life: 1 week in the refrigerator; 3 months in the freezer

3 tbsp groundnut, sunflower or sesame oil

125g (4oz) carrots, sliced into fine julienne

2–6 hot green or red chillies (to taste), deseeded and finely sliced

200g (7oz) shallots or onion, finely sliced

5 large garlic cloves, finely shredded

2.5cm (1 inch) fresh ginger, finely shredded

2 lemongrass stalks, hard outer layers removed, finely chopped

½ tsp turmeric

4–5 kaffir lime leaves, shredded

250ml (8fl oz) Fish Stock (see page 30)

400ml (14fl oz) coconut milk

juice of 1 lime and grated zest of ½ lime

2–3 tbsp Thai fish sauce (*nam pla*), or salt to taste

3 tbsp chopped fresh basil or coriander

1 Heat the oil in a large wok or frying pan. Add the carrots and chillies and stir-fry for 2–3 minutes. Add the shallots, garlic, ginger and lemongrass and stir-fry until all are evenly golden. Add the turmeric and half the kaffir lime leaves and fry for a further 1–2 minutes.

2 Pour in the stock and coconut milk and bring to the boil, then reduce the heat and simmer gently for about 20 minutes or until the liquid has reduced by a quarter and thickened slightly. Add the lime juice and zest and the fish sauce or salt and stir well.

3 To use: add cubed fish or other seafood to the sauce and cook for 5–8 minutes or until the fish is ready. Stir in the remaining kaffir lime leaves and the basil or coriander and serve.

GREEN CURRY PASTE ▷

250g (8oz) shallots, unpeeled

1 large head of garlic, unpeeled

4–6 green chillies (to taste)

2.5cm (1 inch) fresh galangal or ginger, chopped

5 lemongrass stalks, hard outer layers removed, chopped

1 large bunch of fresh coriander (roots, stalks and leaves), coarsely chopped

3–4 tbsp Thai fish sauce (*nam pla*)

1–2 tbsp palm sugar or soft brown sugar

4 tbsp groundnut or sesame oil

1 Place the shallots and garlic on a baking tray and bake in an oven preheated to 220°C/425°F/Gas Mark 7 for 20–25 minutes or until lightly browned and soft to the touch. Leave to cool.

2 Peel the shallots and squeeze the garlic out of its skin.

3 Place the chillies in a pan with just enough water to cover, bring to the boil and simmer for about 10 minutes or until soft. Cool under cold water, then deseed and coarsely chop the chillies.

4 Place the shallots, garlic, chillies and all the remaining ingredients except the oil in a blender (for a smooth paste) or food processor (for a coarser texture) and process. If too dry, add a little water.

5 Heat the oil in a wok or frying pan, add the paste and fry for 5–8 minutes or until most of the liquid has evaporated and the paste has darkened slightly. Leave to cool. The paste can be transferred to sterilized jars, if desired.

6 To use: dilute 12–18 tablespoons (2–3 tablespoons per person) of paste in a pan with 400ml (14fl oz) coconut milk and bring to the boil. Add prawns or other seafood. Reduce the heat and simmer for 10 minutes. If the sauce is too thin, take out the seafood and boil the sauce until thickened.

This popular Thai curry paste is normally prepared in large quantities and used as a base for hot and refreshing prawn or seafood curries, to finish soups and stews and to add instant flavour to many dishes. Traditionally, the recipe includes shrimp paste, an aromatic purée made from fermented shrimps and fish, but you can use fish sauce or anchovy paste instead.

Enough for 500g (1lb) prawns or other seafood

Shelf-life: 2 weeks refrigerated in a tightly sealed jar (make sure there is a protective layer of oil over the paste); 3 months in the freezer; 6 months in a sealed jar (see pages 134–35)

OPPOSITE: STEPS 1, 2, 4 AND 5 OF MAKING GREEN CURRY PASTE

MOLE

Mole is one of the signature sauces of Mexican cuisine. The story goes that it was invented by Spanish nuns in the 18th century, but in fact re-fried pastes of dried chillies combined with purées of fruit, spices, herbs and chocolate had been used by the indigenous population for centuries. Making traditional mole is a very complex process and recipes vary from region to region and even from family to family. This recipe is a simplified version and gives a thick, flavoursome, medium-hot sauce. Mexican ingredients are available in many large supermarkets and specialist shops. The dried chillies give mole its characteristic slightly bitter flavour. Traditionally the sauce is poured over poached turkey, chicken or pork and the cooking liquid is used instead of stock. Serve with lots of soft tortillas to mop up the delicious sauce.

For the paste

2 each of the following dried chillies: ancho, guajillo, pasilla and mulato, hard stems removed, deseeded

1 dried chipotle chilli, deseeded

1 onion, unpeeled

1 head of garlic, unpeeled

4 plum tomatoes or other cooking tomatoes

2 stale tortillas or 1 thick slice of white bread, cut into chunks

1 ripe plantain or banana, peeled

For the spice mix

5–6 allspice berries

2–3 cloves

2.5cm (1 inch) cinnamon stick or cassia, crumbled

For the mole

4 tbsp olive oil or lard

75g (2½oz) raisins, plumped in a little boiling water for 20 minutes

30g (1oz) blanched almonds, browned in a little oil, then ground

30g (1oz) sesame or pumpkin seeds, browned in a little oil, then ground (reserve some whole seeds for garnish)

1 tsp dried oregano

1 tsp dried thyme

50g (1¾oz) dark, unsweetened chocolate or 2 tbsp unsweetened cocoa powder

600ml (1 pint) Chicken Stock (see page 28)

salt

1 For the paste, place the chillies, onion, garlic, tomatoes and tortillas or bread on a well-greased baking tray and roast in an oven preheated to 220°C/425°F/Gas Mark 7. Remove the chillies after about 2–3 minutes; they should be fragrant and starting to change colour. Place them in a bowl, cover with boiling water and leave to soak for 30 minutes.

2 Remove the tortillas or bread when lightly browned but roast the onion, garlic and tomatoes until soft, a further 20 minutes or so.

3 Drain the chillies (but taste the soaking liquid and, if not too bitter, reserve it) and purée in a blender or food processor. Add the plantain or banana and the roasted ingredients and process to a smooth paste. If too dry, add a few tablespoons of water, stock or the chilli soaking liquid.

4 Dry-roast and grind the spice mix (see page 78).

5 Heat the oil or lard in a large pan, add the paste, the spice mix and all the remaining ingredients except the chocolate or cocoa powder, the stock and salt. Fry for 8–10 minutes over a medium heat, stirring constantly and scraping the bottom of the pan, until most of the liquid has evaporated.

6 Add the chocolate or cocoa powder and stir until melted and well mixed in. Stir in the stock, bring to the boil and simmer for about 8–10 minutes or until the sauce thickly coats the back of a spoon. Add salt to taste and garnish with the reserved sesame or pumpkin seeds.

7 To use: pour over poached or roast turkey, chicken or pork and heat through before serving.

Advance preparation: the spice paste keeps for 1 week in the refrigerator and 3 months in the freezer

Shelf-life: 1 week in the refrigerator; 3 months in the freezer

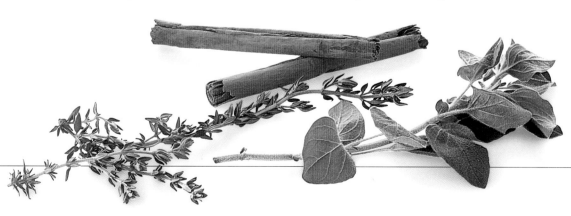

CHILLI CON CARNE

This internationally renowned dish was invented by Mexican farm workers in the wilds of south-west America in the middle of the last century. Flavoured with chilli, cumin and tomatoes, it is a substantial meal in itself, with all the fire of Mexican food. Mixed with generous amounts of melted Monterey Jack or Cheddar cheese, it can be served as a dip with tortillas or as a filling for enchiladas and soft tortillas. It goes with hamburgers and, of course, rice.

Serves 8–10

Shelf-life: *1 week in the refrigerator; 3 months in the freezer*

4–6 dried red chillies such as ancho or New Mexico red, hard stems removed, deseeded, or chilli powder to taste
4 tbsp olive oil
½–1 tsp cumin seeds
2 onions, chopped
8 fat garlic cloves, finely chopped
2–3 tsp dried oregano
750g (1½lb) lean beef, minced or finely chopped
2 x 200g (7oz) tins of tomatoes
2–3 generous tbsp tomato purée
2 x 400g (13oz) tins of red kidney beans, or 250g (8oz) dried kidney beans, cooked
chilli powder to taste
5 tbsp chopped fresh coriander
salt

1 Place the chillies in a small pan, pour over boiling water to cover and simmer until the skins begin to split and the chillies are soft, about 20 minutes. Drain, reserving about 150ml (¼ pint) of the water if it is not too bitter. Transfer the chillies to a blender or food processor and process to a smooth purée with the reserved water or other water if that is too bitter.

2 Heat the oil in a heavy pan, add the cumin seeds, onions, garlic and oregano and fry until the onions start to brown. Add the meat and stir well to break it up. Reduce the heat, cover and cook for about 15–20 minutes, stirring frequently, until the meat is tender and most of the liquid has evaporated.

3 Add the tomatoes with their juices, the chilli purée and the tomato purée and bring to the boil. Reduce the heat and simmer, half covered, for about 30 minutes, stirring frequently. Add the kidney beans and salt to taste and continue cooking for 30–45 minutes, or until the sauce has reduced and is quite thick. Taste the chilli and add some chilli powder, if desired. Sprinkle with the coriander and serve.

MANCHAMANTEL

3 dried ancho chillies, deseeded
2 dried mulato chillies, deseeded
6 tbsp olive oil or lard
1 small onion, coarsely chopped
4 garlic cloves, coarsely chopped
3 ripe bananas, coarsely chopped
500g (1lb) plum tomatoes, peeled and deseeded (see page 43)
2 tsp ground cinnamon
¼ tsp ground cloves
¼ tsp ground allspice
2 tbsp dried oregano
salt

1 Place the chillies on a baking sheet and roast in an oven preheated to 220°C/425°F/Gas Mark 7 for 2–3 minutes, until fragrant. Transfer the chillies to a bowl, cover with boiling water and leave to soak for 30 minutes. Drain well, reserving the soaking liquid if it is not too bitter.

2 Heat 4 tablespoons of the olive oil or lard in a frying pan, add the onion, garlic and bananas and fry for 10–15 minutes, until nicely browned.

3 Put the banana mixture, chillies and tomatoes in a blender or food processor and process to a smooth purée. Add a little of the chilli soaking liquid or water to ease the processing if the mixture is too dry.

4 Heat the remaining oil or lard in a deep frying pan and add the cinnamon, cloves, allspice and oregano. Add the purée and fry, stirring occasionally, for 5–8 minutes or until the sauce has thickened and most of the liquid has evaporated. Season with salt to taste.

5 To use: add cubed and browned beef or lamb to the sauce and simmer until tender. Add a few tablespoons of water while cooking if it is too dry.

Sweet, hot and intense in flavour, this dark-red sauce originates in central Mexico, where its name literally means tablecloth stainer. It can be made from other fruit instead of bananas, such as pineapple, mango or papaya.

Enough for about 500–750g (1–1½lb) beef or lamb

Shelf-life: *3 weeks in the refrigerator; 3 months in the freezer*

PASTA SAUCES

THESE EASY, DELICIOUS and healthy sauces are popular with many busy cooks because they are so quick to make. Some of them are classics but I have also included modern takes on old favourites. What they all have in common is their lively flavour and their reliance on a combination of storecupboard ingredients and fresh produce.

PASSATA

A versatile tomato sauce that can be used as a base for many dishes. I make it in large quantities whenever ripe cooking tomatoes are available, as it can be frozen or bottled very successfully. For a spicier version, add fresh or dried chilli to taste. If you prefer a smooth sauce, don't peel the tomatoes – simply sieve the finished sauce. Add a little sugar if the tomatoes are tart.

Makes 1.5 litres (2½ pints)

Shelf-life: 1 week in the refrigerator; 3 months in the freezer; 6 months in sealed jars (see pages 134–35)

125ml (4fl oz) olive oil
500g (1lb) onions, chopped
6 garlic cloves, chopped
2kg (4lb) plum or cooking tomatoes, peeled, deseeded (see page 43) and chopped
a bouquet garni made with a few sprigs of parsley and oregano, a few celery leaves, a bay leaf and 1 strip of lemon zest (optional) (see page 30)
2 tsp sugar (optional)
salt and freshly ground black pepper

Heat the oil in a large pan, add the onions and garlic and fry over a medium heat until the onions are translucent. Add the tomatoes and the bouquet garni, if using, and simmer for about an hour, or until most of the liquid has evaporated. Fish out the bouquet garni, then taste the sauce and add sugar, if necessary, and salt and pepper.

ARRABBIATA

6 tbsp olive oil
1–3 tsp dried chilli flakes (to taste)
4 garlic cloves, coarsely chopped
500g (1lb) plum or cooking tomatoes, peeled, deseeded (see page 43) and chopped
1 tsp sugar (optional)
3 tbsp chopped fresh flat-leaf parsley
salt

This spicy tomato sauce can be served on pasta (traditionally penne) or poured over freshly grilled steaks, chops or grilled or roasted vegetables.

Shelf-life: 1 week in the refrigerator; 3 months in the freezer; 6 months in sealed jars (see pages 134–35)

Heat the oil in a large frying pan, add the chilli flakes and garlic and fry for 4–5 minutes, or until the garlic starts to turn golden. Add the tomatoes and simmer, stirring from time to time, until they have begun to disintegrate and the sauce has thickened, about 15 minutes. Taste the sauce and add sugar if necessary, then stir in the parsley and season to taste with salt.

AUBERGINE SAUCE

Aubergine makes a delicious, versatile sauce that can be served with pasta, noodles, rice or other cooked grains. I sometimes add 2 tablespoons of soy sauce, which gives an extra flavour dimension.

Advance preparation: the passata can be made in advance

Shelf-life: 1 week in the refrigerator; 3 months in the freezer

2 tsp salt
250g (8oz) aubergine, cut into 1cm (½ inch) cubes
3 tbsp olive oil
1 large onion, chopped
4 garlic cloves, chopped
2 tbsp dark soy sauce
150ml (¼ pint) Passata (see above) or 3 tbsp bought tomato purée diluted with 100ml (3½ fl oz) water
250g (8oz) plum or cooking tomatoes, peeled, deseeded (see page 43) and chopped
3 tbsp chopped fresh thyme or oregano
salt and freshly ground black pepper

1 Sprinkle the salt over the aubergine in a colander and set aside to drain for about 30 minutes. Pat dry with kitchen paper.

2 Heat the oil in a large frying pan, add the onion and garlic and fry until the onion starts to colour, about 5–8 minutes. Add the aubergine and fry until it softens a little. Add the soy sauce and fry until it is absorbed, then add the passata or the diluted tomato purée. Cover the sauce and simmer until the aubergine is very soft, about 10 minutes.

3 Stir in the tomatoes and thyme or oregano, heat through and season to taste with salt and freshly ground black pepper.

TOMATO & TUNA SAUCE

A Mediterranean pasta sauce that is robust in flavour and very easy to prepare.

Shelf-life: *1 week in the refrigerator; 3 months in the freezer; 6 months in sealed jars (see pages 134–35)*

4 tbsp olive oil

1 tsp fennel seeds (optional)

1 large onion, chopped

3 garlic cloves, chopped

4 anchovy fillets, chopped

500g (1lb) plum or cooking tomatoes, peeled, deseeded (see page 43) and chopped

2 tbsp bought tomato purée, diluted in 100ml (3½ fl oz) red or white wine, stock or water

a bouquet garni made with a few sprigs of fresh thyme, fennel leaves and parsley and 2 strips of lemon zest (see page 30)

1 x 200g (7oz) tin of tuna, in brine or oil, drained and crumbled

2 tbsp capers, rinsed and coarsely chopped (left whole if small)

3 tbsp chopped fresh flat-leaf parsley or 2 tbsp chopped fresh lemon thyme or tarragon

salt, if necessary, and freshly ground black pepper

1 Heat the oil in a large frying pan, add the fennel seeds, if using, and fry for 2–3 minutes, or until they begin to give off a pleasant spicy aroma. Stir in the onion and garlic and fry until the onion has started to colour, about 5 minutes. Add the anchovies and stir until they start to break up.

2 Add the tomatoes, the diluted tomato purée and the bouquet garni, bring to the boil, then reduce the heat and simmer until most of the liquid has evaporated, about 30 minutes.

3 Stir in the tuna, capers and the parsley, lemon thyme or tarragon. Season to taste and simmer for a further 2–3 minutes.

TOMATO & GRILLED COURGETTE SAUCE

2 tsp salt

250g (8oz) courgettes, cut into slices 2cm (¾ inch) thick

6 tbsp olive oil

150g (5oz) shallots, quartered

6 garlic cloves, quartered

500g (1lb) plum or cooking tomatoes, peeled, deseeded (see page 43) and chopped

2 tbsp bought tomato purée, diluted in 100ml (3½fl oz) red or white wine, stock or water

a bouquet garni made with a few sprigs of thyme, rosemary and parsley and 2 strips of orange zest (see page 30)

2 tbsp chopped fresh thyme or 3 tbsp chopped fresh flat-leaf parsley

salt and freshly ground black pepper

1 Sprinkle the salt over the courgettes in a colander and set aside to drain for 30 minutes. Pat dry with kitchen paper.

2 Heat 4 tablespoons of the oil in a large frying pan, add the shallots and garlic and fry until golden, about 7–8 minutes. Add the tomatoes, the diluted tomato purée and the bouquet garni and bring to the boil. Reduce the heat and simmer for about 30 minutes or until most of the liquid has evaporated.

3 Brush the courgettes with the remaining oil and cook either on a ridged grill pan or under a hot grill until nicely browned on both sides. Add to the sauce together with the thyme or parsley and salt and pepper and simmer for 3–4 minutes.

Roasting or grilling the courgettes keeps them fresh and crunchy. Pour this sauce over tagliatelle, pappardelle or any other flat ribbon pasta and serve with plenty of grated Parmesan.

Shelf-life: *1 week in the refrigerator; 3 months in the freezer; 6 months in sealed jars (see pages 134–35)*

VONGOLE

My friend Brad gave me this recipe – it is the easiest and most effective way of making this Italian classic. It differs slightly from the traditional vongole in that the tomatoes are just heated through rather than cooked.

Shelf-life: *1 week in the refrigerator*

6–8 tbsp good olive oil
1–2 tbsp dried chilli flakes
4 garlic cloves, chopped
1 x 290g (9¼oz) tin of littleneck clams, drained
250g (8oz) plum or cooking tomatoes, peeled, deseeded (see page 43) and finely chopped
a small bunch of fresh flat-leaf parsley or basil, roughly torn
salt and freshly ground black pepper

Heat the oil in a large frying pan, add the chilli and fry over a high heat for 2–3 minutes. Add the garlic and fry until it starts to colour. Stir in the clams, turning them in the oil to heat through, then add the tomatoes and stir until the sauce is hot. Season to taste and stir in the herbs.

THREE-TOMATO SAUCE

This pasta sauce is also delicious served with grilled, fried or barbecued chicken. Sun-dried tomatoes in oil are not suitable for this recipe; use the dried variety in packets instead.

Advance preparation: *the passata can be made in advance*

Shelf-life: *1 week in the refrigerator; 3 months in the freezer; 6 months in sealed jars (see pages 134–35)*

4 tbsp olive oil
4 garlic cloves, thinly sliced
500ml (17fl oz) Passata (see page 90)
250ml (8fl oz) red wine
100g (3½oz) sun-dried tomatoes, soaked in hot water for 20 minutes, then drained and sliced into fine julienne
250g (8oz) cherry or baby plum tomatoes
a small bunch of fresh basil, torn
salt and freshly ground black pepper

1 Heat the oil in a large frying pan, add the garlic and fry until it turns golden. Add the passata, wine and sun-dried tomatoes and bring to the boil, then reduce the heat and simmer until reduced by a third, about 20 minutes.

2 Roast the cherry or baby plum tomatoes in a very hot oven or on a dry frying pan until lightly charred and soft. Fold them into the sauce with the basil, then season to taste with salt and freshly ground black pepper.

WILD MUSHROOM SAUCE

3 tbsp olive oil
1 large onion, chopped
2 garlic cloves, chopped
250g (8oz) shiitake mushrooms, hard stems removed, sliced
250g (8oz) oyster mushrooms, torn into pieces
15g (½oz) dried porcini, soaked in 75ml (2½fl oz) hot water for 20 minutes, drained, soaking liquid reserved
1 tbsp dark soy sauce
350ml (12fl oz) Chicken or Vegetable Stock (see pages 28 and 31)
150ml (¼ pint) white wine
2 tbsp chopped fresh thyme or oregano
75g (2½oz) butter, chilled and cubed (optional)
salt and freshly ground black pepper

A real favourite of mine, this pasta sauce is quite a luxury. Experiment with different varieties of mushroom depending on what is available.

Advance preparation: *the stock can be made in advance*

Shelf-life: *1 week in the refrigerator*

1 Heat the oil in a large frying pan, add the onion and garlic and fry until golden. Add all the mushrooms, including the porcini, and the soy sauce and fry until the mushrooms are limp.

2 Strain the porcini soaking liquid and add to the pan with the stock and wine. Simmer for about 30 minutes, or until most of the liquid has evaporated and the sauce has thickened.

3 Add the thyme or oregano and, if an extra-rich flavour is preferred, beat in the butter a little at a time. Season to taste.

VARIATION

CREAMY MUSHROOM SAUCE
Substitute 350g (11½oz) finely sliced button mushrooms for the wild mushrooms and omit the soy sauce. Use 150ml (¼ pint) chicken or vegetable stock or white wine instead of the 350ml (12fl oz) chicken stock and 150ml (¼ pint) white wine. Simmer for about 15 minutes, then stir in 250ml (8fl oz) double cream or crème fraîche and bubble, stirring continuously, for 3–4 minutes. Remove from the heat and instead of the herbs and butter, stir in 4–5 shredded sage leaves and 1 tablespoon lemon juice.

OPPOSITE, CLOCKWISE FROM TOP LEFT: VONGOLE with pasta shells, THREE-TOMATO SAUCE with pappardelle, CREAMY MUSHROOM SAUCE with riccioli pasta

SALSAS & OTHER FRESH SAUCES

FRESH SAUCES SUCH AS SALSAS, CHUTNEYS, RAITAS AND SAMBALS ARE EXTREMELY VERSATILE AND REQUIRE

VERY LITTLE PREPARATION OR COOKING. YOU CAN USE THEM TO ENLIVEN THE SIMPLEST OF MEALS — TRY PILING

THEM OVER GRILLED FISH, MEAT OR CHEESE, OR MIXING THEM INTO PASTA, FOR EXAMPLE. DIPS CAN BE

SERVED WITH PITTA BREAD OR RAW VEGETABLES OR AS A LIGHT SNACK WITH A GLASS OF WINE.

SALSAS

THE WORD SALSA describes a large family of fresh or cooked salad-like relishes, usually flavoured with chilli and herbs. In Mexico, where the salsa evolved, they vary greatly in heat and spiciness, from the mild to the dangerously hot. Salsas can be served immediately but are much improved if left to marinate for a few hours.

THREE-CHILLI SALSA

If you love chillies, this salsa is a must. Probably the hottest recipe in the book, this tart and fragrant salsa can be served piled on top of grilled fish or chicken or just as a dip with tortilla chips or crudités.

Shelf-life: 1 week in the refrigerator

100g (3½oz) mild red chillies, such as Anaheim, cubanelle or fresno, roasted, peeled and deseeded (see page 96), sliced

2–3 red or green jalapeño chillies, deseeded and thinly sliced

2–3 chipotle chillies, soaked in hot water for 25 minutes, drained, deseeded and chopped

250g (8oz) tomatoes, peeled, deseeded (see page 45) and chopped

2 limes, peeled and segments removed, chopped

strained juice and grated zest of 1 lime

4 tbsp chopped fresh coriander leaves

salt

Mix all the ingredients together and leave to marinate in the refrigerator for 1 hour before serving.

TOMATO & CUCUMBER SALSA ▷

250g (8oz) large tomatoes, cubed

250g (8oz) small, firm cucumbers, unpeeled, cubed

1 large red or white onion, finely chopped

1–2 green chillies, deseeded and finely chopped

1 tbsp chopped fresh marjoram, or 2 tsp dried

3–4 tbsp chopped fresh flat-leaf parsley or mint

3–4 tbsp olive oil

strained juice of 1 lemon or to taste

salt

This brightly coloured salsa is based on a traditional Arab salad. I serve this on a mound of hot burghul or rice pilaff. It is also delicious with fish or chicken or as a tasty side salad.

Mix all the ingredients together in a bowl and leave to marinate in the refrigerator for at least 1 hour.

OPPOSITE: FRESH TOMATO & CUCUMBER SALSA BEING TOSSED IN A BOWL

TOMATO & PEPPER SALSA

Serve this with any grilled meat or vegetables, as a piquant salad or with pasta. You can make it in a food processor but be careful not to overprocess – the vegetables should be finely chopped, not puréed. For a coarser texture, chop the ingredients by hand. For an extra smoky flavour, roast and peel the peppers (see below). The peppers can be replaced with avocado, banana, cucumber or even chopped mango.

Shelf-life: *1 week in the refrigerator; 6 months in sealed jars*

750g (1½lb) mixed green, red and yellow peppers, deseeded and coarsely chopped

2–3 fresh red or green chillies, deseeded and coarsely chopped

1 large red onion, coarsely chopped

2 garlic cloves, peeled

3 tbsp olive oil, corn oil or groundnut oil

3 tbsp red wine vinegar or lemon juice

2 tsp salt

500g (1lb) firm, ripe tomatoes, peeled, deseeded (see page 43) and finely chopped

3 tbsp chopped fresh coriander or flat-leaf parsley (optional)

1 Put all the ingredients except the tomatoes and coriander or parsley in a food processor and process, starting and stopping the machine, until the mixture is finely chopped but not puréed.

2 Transfer the mixture to a bowl and mix in the tomatoes and the coriander or parsley, if using. If you are bottling the salsa, transfer the mixture to a pan and simmer for 5 minutes before packing into sterilized jars (see pages 134–35).

3 Otherwise, leave to marinate in the refrigerator for 1 hour before serving.

PEELING PEPPERS & CHILLIES

Either grill the peppers or chillies on a dry heavy-based frying pan or griddle or roast over an open flame or in an oven until charred. Put them in a plastic bag for 5 minutes, then remove from the bag, hold under cold running water and peel off the skin.

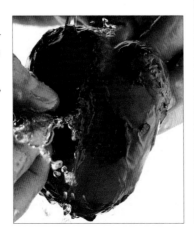

PAPAYA & KAFFIR LIME SALSA

1 green papaya, peeled, deseeded and coarsely grated

1–2 red Thai chillies, finely chopped

3 tbsp coconut cream

150ml (¼ pint) coconut milk

4–5 kaffir lime leaves, finely chopped

strained juice of 1 large lime

grated zest of ½ lime

1–2 tsp palm sugar, jaggery (crushed) or light brown sugar

1–2 tbsp Thai fish sauce (*nam pla*)

2 tbsp coarsely chopped fresh coriander

Green papaya is a surprising taste sensation – it adds a fresh and delicate flavour and crunchy texture to this salsa, which is particularly good served with smoked fish. Green papayas are available from Indian and Chinese food shops but, if you can't find them, unripe, green mango or a sour apple can be substituted.

Shelf-life: *3–4 days in the refrigerator*

Mix all the ingredients together in a bowl, cover and refrigerate for at least 2 hours before serving.

VARIATION

EXOTIC PAPAYA & KAFFIR LIME SALSA
Add 6 anchovy fillets, drained and cut into strips, or 100g (3½oz) rinsed and chopped salted herrings to the finished salsa. Serve as an accompaniment to chicken or fish.

BEETROOT & APPLE SALSA

250g (8oz) raw or cooked beetroot, coarsely grated

200g (7oz) apple, cored and cubed

1 onion, finely chopped

100g (3½oz) gherkins, chopped

4 tbsp red wine vinegar

2 tbsp mild olive, groundnut or sesame oil

1 tsp sugar

3 tbsp chopped fresh dill or flat-leaf parsley

salt and freshly ground black pepper

A fresh and delicious salsa that is good with cold cuts, pickled herrings or cheese. If you don't like raw beetroot, either boil it for about 45 minutes or, which I much prefer, roast it in an oven until soft.

Shelf-life: *3–4 days in the refrigerator*

See page 21 for illustration

Mix all the ingredients together in a bowl and leave to marinate in the refrigerator for at least 1 hour before serving.

TOMATILLO SALSA

Tomatillos, sometimes called jamberries or Mexican green tomatoes, are available either fresh or tinned in Mexican food shops and are a relative of the cape gooseberry (which can be substituted in this recipe). Some cooks remove the small seeds but I think they add an interesting and unique texture to the salsa.

Shelf-life: *3–4 days in the refrigerator*

500g (1lb) tomatillos, husks removed, cubed

2–4 jalapeño chillies, roasted, peeled and deseeded (see opposite), finely chopped

1 white or yellow onion, finely chopped

strained juice of 2 limes and grated zest to taste

3 tbsp light olive oil or groundnut oil

1–2 tbsp chopped fresh coriander or flat-leaf parsley

salt

Mix all the ingredients together and leave to marinate in the refrigerator for at least 1 hour before serving.

POMEGRANATE & HERB SALSA

This is the simplest of salsas, wonderfully sharp and fresh in flavour. It is found in both Mexican and Persian cuisines and is superb with simple grilled fish.

Shelf-life: *1 week in the refrigerator*

See pages 15 and 99 for illustrations

1½ bunches each of fresh mint, flat-leaf parsley (leaves only) and coriander, coarsely chopped

seeds of 1 pomegranate (see below)

1 small white onion, finely chopped

6 tbsp lime juice

grated zest of ½ lime

1–2 jalapeño or serrano chillies, finely chopped

2 tbsp groundnut oil or olive oil

salt

Mix all the ingredients together in a bowl. Cover and chill for about 1 hour.

GUACAMOLE

3 ripe avocados, halved, stone removed

1 white or red onion, finely chopped

1 beef or other large tomato, or 2 plum tomatoes, peeled, deseeded (see page 43) and finely chopped

strained juice of 2 lemons or 4 limes, or to taste

grated lemon or lime zest to taste

1–3 fresh red chillies, deseeded and finely chopped

1–2 tbsp chopped fresh coriander leaves (optional)

salt

Scoop the avocado flesh into a bowl and mash coarsely with a fork, then mix in the rest of the ingredients. Squeeze a little more lemon or lime juice over the guacamole to prevent it going brown, then cover and refrigerate for about 30 minutes before serving.

The classic Mexican salsa. Use only completely ripe avocados, making sure you scrape out as much of the flesh as possible. I prefer my guacamole coarse in texture, but for smoother results use a food processor.

Shelf-life: *3–4 days in the refrigerator*

REMOVING THE SEEDS FROM A POMEGRANATE

1 Using a sharp knife, top and tail the pomegranate.

2 Make 4 equidistant cuts from the top to the bottom of the fruit.

3 Twist the pomegranate to break it into halves, then into quarters.

4 Prise away the seeds, discarding any of the bitter membrane.

MIXED PEPPER SALSA

Colourful, refreshing and incredibly tasty, this salsa is easily made in a food processor, but can look stunning if the ingredients are chopped by hand. Try chopping the peppers into julienne or matchsticks for really spectacular results.

Shelf-life: *3–4 days in the refrigerator*

1 large red pepper, roasted, peeled and deseeded (see page 96)

1 large yellow or orange pepper, roasted, peeled and deseeded (see page 96)

1 large green pepper, roasted, peeled and deseeded (see page 96)

1 white or purple onion, finely chopped

1–3 jalapeño or Anaheim chillies, roasted, peeled and deseeded (see page 96)

6 tbsp lime juice or white wine vinegar

3–4 tbsp olive oil

3 tbsp shredded fresh coriander leaves

salt

1 Put the peppers, onion and chilli in a food processor and process, starting and stopping the machine, until the mixture is finely chopped but not puréed.

2 Transfer the mixture to a bowl and add the rest of the ingredients. Mix well, cover and chill before serving.

CITRUS SALSA

A tart and refreshing salsa with a hint of chilli. I serve this with grilled or fried fish.

Shelf-life: *3–4 days in the refrigerator*

2 oranges, peeled and segments removed, cut into 1cm (½ inch) pieces

2 large lemons, peeled and segments removed, cut into 1cm (½ inch) pieces

2 pickled lemons, deseeded and finely chopped

1½ tsp chilli flakes, or more to taste

2 tbsp sweet paprika or other sweet pimiento powder

3 tbsp chopped fresh flat-leaf parsley or mint

salt

Mix all the ingredients together in a bowl and leave to marinate in the refrigerator for at least 1 hour before serving.

MANGO & TOMATO SALSA

1 ripe, firm mango, peeled, stoned and cubed

300g (10oz) plum or beef tomatoes, peeled (see page 43) and finely chopped

1 small white onion, finely chopped

2 garlic cloves, crushed

1–2 red chillies, finely chopped

5 tbsp lemon juice

grated zest of ½ lemon

2–3 tbsp torn fresh mint or a mixture of mint and basil

1–2 tsp honey or sugar

salt

A fragrant, sweet and sour salsa that is fantastic with chicken. This is just as delicious if you substitute papaya for the mango.

Shelf-life: *1 week in the refrigerator*

Mix all the ingredients in a bowl. Cover and chill well before serving.

ROAST CORN SALSA

2 ears of corn

400g (13oz) plum tomatoes, roasted, peeled and deseeded (see page 43), finely chopped

2 jalapeño chillies, roasted, peeled and deseeded (see page 96), finely chopped

1 red onion, finely chopped

1 garlic clove, crushed

2–3 tbsp olive oil

juice of 1 lemon

grated zest of ½ lemon

1–2 tbsp torn fresh coriander

salt

A wonderfully smoky-flavoured salsa that makes the perfect accompaniment to hamburgers. You could use frozen corn instead of fresh: simply roast it on a baking sheet in a hot oven until it starts to colour.

Shelf-life: *3–4 days in the refrigerator*

1 Grill or barbecue the corn for 20–30 minutes, or until golden. Cut the top off each ear of corn and stand it cut-side down on a chopping board. With a sharp knife, cut away the kernels, using the hard cob as a guide.

2 Put the kernels in a bowl and add the rest of the ingredients. Mix well, then cover and refrigerate for at least 2 hours before serving.

OPPOSITE, CLOCKWISE FROM TOP LEFT: MIXED PEPPER SALSA, MANGO & TOMATO SALSA, ROAST CORN SALSA AND POMEGRANATE & HERB SALSA (SEE PAGE 97)

FRESH CHUTNEYS

IN INDIA, THE WORD CHUTNEY refers to a wide range of condiments from slow-cooked, jam-like preserves to more simple relishes made from freshly chopped raw vegetables that are ready to eat after marinating for a few hours. Chutneys can add spice to snacks, cool down hot curries or make an unusual sauce for rice or pasta.

FRESH ONION CHUTNEY

Select juicy, sweet salad onions for this fresh and simple chutney. Serve it as a side salad, to accompany poppadoms or crisps, or even as an interesting sandwich filling.

Shelf-life: 1 day in the refrigerator

500g (1lb) large red or white sweet onions, sliced into thin rings

1 tbsp salt

1–2 green or red chillies, deseeded and finely chopped

3 tbsp white wine vinegar or cider vinegar

2 tbsp chopped fresh mint or coriander

1 tsp nigella seeds, dry-roasted (see page 78) (optional)

1 Put the onion rings in a colander and sprinkle with the salt. Mix well and leave to drain for about 1 hour. Rinse, then queeze any remaining moisture from the onions with your hands and pat dry.

2 Mix the rest of the ingredients together in a bowl, add the onions and leave to stand for about 1 hour before serving.

COCONUT CHUTNEY

1 tbsp blue poppy seeds, dry-roasted (see page 78)

1 coconut, flesh removed and finely grated or rasped, or 250g (8oz) unsweetened desiccated coconut, soaked in water for 20 minutes, then drained and squeezed dry

2.5cm (1 inch) fresh ginger, finely grated

1 small bunch of fresh coriander, finely chopped

1 tbsp jaggery, crushed, or sugar (optional)

1–2 green chillies, deseeded and finely chopped

200ml (7fl oz) coconut milk

strained lime or lemon juice to taste

salt

In southern India this chutney is made fresh daily. For a whiter, less fibrous chutney, remove the brown skin from the coconut flesh with a sharp knife or a potato peeler. If fresh coconut is not available, use unsweetened desiccated coconut or frozen shredded coconut, which is available in some Indian shops. Coconut chutney is the traditional accompaniment to samosas.

Shelf-life: 1 week in the refrigerator

Mix all the ingredients together in a bowl and marinate for 1 hour before serving.

HERB CHUTNEY

The essence of spring and summer, this refreshing chutney is full of vitality. Try other fresh herbs such as flat-leaf parsley and dill – if using mint, use only the leaves and discard the tough stems.

1 large bunch of fresh mint or coriander, chopped

1 bunch of spring onions, finely chopped

1 tbsp sugar

1–2 green or red chillies, deseeded and finely chopped

1 garlic clove, crushed

strained juice of 1–2 limes, or to taste

1/2 tsp chilli powder, or to taste

salt

Mix all the ingredients together in a bowl and leave to marinate in the refrigerator for no longer than an hour before serving– this is best eaten fresh.

CASHEW NUT CHUTNEY

200g (7oz) cashew nuts

1 small onion, chopped

3 tbsp fresh coriander

2.5cm (1 inch) fresh ginger, chopped

2–3 green chillies, deseeded and finely chopped

1/4 tsp chilli powder

1–2 tbsp lemon or lime juice (to taste)

salt

Traditionally the ingredients for this chutney were pulverized in a stone pestle and mortar or with a grinding stone. Using a food processor is the modern equivalent but the flavour is less intense and the texture different. For a nuttier flavour, roast the cashew nuts until golden.

Shelf-life: 1 week in the refrigerator

Put the cashew nuts, onion, coriander and ginger in a food processor and process until smooth. Transfer to a bowl and stir in the remaining ingredients. Leave to marinate in the refrigerator for an hour.

GREEN CHILLI CHUTNEY

Try this delicious, fresh-tasting, medium-hot chutney with vegetarian food or grilled or fried fish.

Shelf-life: *3 weeks in the refrigerator; 1 month in sealed jars*

300g (10oz) long, thin, green chillies, stems removed, sliced in half lengthways
3 tbsp salt
8 garlic cloves, peeled
2.5cm (1 inch) fresh ginger
3 tbsp white mustard seeds
1 tbsp cumin seeds
1/4 tsp asafoetida (optional)
100ml (3 1/2 fl oz) mustard oil, sesame oil or groundnut oil
1 tsp turmeric
1 tsp nigella seeds, dry-roasted (see page 78)
100g (3 1/2 fl oz) tamarind pulp soaked in 200ml (7fl oz) hot vinegar, sieved (see page 124)
3 tbsp jaggery, crushed, or brown sugar
salt

1 Place the chillies in a colander and sprinkle with the salt. Leave to cure for about 3–4 hours. Wash off the excess salt, drain and pat dry with kitchen paper.

2 Place the garlic, ginger, mustard seeds, cumin and asafoetida, if using, in a spice mill or food processor and process to a smooth paste.

3 Heat the oil in a pan, add the turmeric and nigella and fry for 2–3 minutes, or until the mixture starts to emit a delicious spicy aroma. Add the paste and fry for 5–8 minutes, until the mixture starts to brown. Add the tamarind vinegar, the jaggery or brown sugar and salt and simmer for a further 5–8 minutes, stirring and scraping the base of the pan until most of the liquid has evaporated.

4 Add the chillies, stir well and simmer for 3–4 minutes. The chutney can be packed into sterilized bottles or jars at this point (see pages 134–35).

CARROT CHUTNEY

400g (13oz) carrots, coarsely grated
2 tsp salt
75g (2 1/2 oz) pistachio nuts, roasted in a dry pan until golden, finely chopped
1 bunch of spring onions, finely chopped
5cm (2 inches) fresh ginger, grated
1 tbsp honey or brown sugar (optional)
100g (3 1/2 oz) tamarind pulp, soaked in 100ml (3 1/2 fl oz) hot water, sieved (see page 124)
1–2 red chillies, finely chopped
2 tsp nigella seeds, dry-roasted (see page 78)
3 tbsp chopped fresh dill or mint

1 Place the carrots in a colander, sprinkle with the salt and leave to drain for 1 hour. Rinse in cold water and drain well.

2 In a bowl, mix the carrots with all the remaining ingredients except the dill or mint. Add more salt, if necessary, then leave to marinate in the refrigerator for at least 1 hour. Sprinkle with the dill or mint just before serving.

Crunchy and refreshing, this chutney is especially good with hot curries such as vindaloo or madras. If a sweeter chutney is preferred, increase the amount of honey or sugar.

Shelf-life: *1 week in the refrigerator*

BANANA CHUTNEY

strained juice of 3 limes
1/4 tsp chilli powder
1 garlic clove, crushed
1/4 tsp ground cardamom
1/4 tsp asafoetida
3 ripe bananas, peeled and chopped
2.5cm (1 inch) fresh ginger, grated
1 bunch of spring onions, finely chopped
2 limes, peeled and segments removed, chopped
1–2 chillies, deseeded and finely chopped
salt

Mix the lime juice, chilli powder, garlic, cardamom and asafoetida together in a bowl. Stir in the rest of the ingredients, then cover and marinate for at least 1 hour before serving.

Novel and surprisingly delicious, this classic south Indian chutney goes particularly well with fried or Tandoori chicken (see page 110). You can also make it with ripe plantains.

Shelf-life: *1 week in the refrigerator*

RELISHES

RELISHES MAKE EASY WORK of cooking. Sweet, sour, fiery or mellow, a spoonful of good relish will add interest to any dish. Serve them with hamburgers or barbecued meats, use to enliven sandwiches and cold meat or just as a versatile flavouring for sauces, mayonnaise and soups. I have given large quantities for these relishes as they are easily bottled and stored for future use. I often make big batches of relish on rainy afternoons.

MATBUCHA

A wonderfully tasty relish of Middle Eastern origin. Many other vegetables can be included – try adding chopped courgettes, pumpkin, squash or aubergine along with the peppers. If using tinned tomatoes, always taste and adjust the sweet-sour balance by adding sugar, lemon juice or vinegar to your liking.

Makes 1.5kg (3lb)

Shelf-life: 3 weeks in the refrigerator; 6 months in sealed jars

200ml (7fl oz) good olive oil
1 tbsp cumin seeds or fennel seeds
2 large onions, chopped
1 large head of garlic, peeled and coarsely chopped
1 small head of young celery with its leaves, finely chopped
4 red or green peppers, deseeded and cut into thin ribbons
75–150g (2½–5oz) fresh red chillies, such as red jalapeño, deseeded and chopped
1.5kg (3lb) cooking tomatoes, peeled, deseeded (see page 43) and coarsely chopped, or 3kg (6lb) tinned tomatoes, drained and squeezed
3 tbsp tomato purée
lemon juice to taste (optional)
1 tbsp sugar (optional)
salt

1 Heat the oil in a large pan. Add the cumin or fennel seeds and fry for 2–3 minutes, or until they give off a pleasant nutty aroma. Add the onions, garlic and celery and fry gently for about 8 minutes, or until the onions are translucent, then add the peppers and chillies and fry for a further 5 minutes.

2 Add the tomatoes and tomato purée. Reduce the heat and, with the pan partially covered, simmer, stirring from time to time, for about 1½ hours, or until most of the liquid has evaporated and the relish has thickened. Taste, then stir in some lemon juice and the sugar, if necessary, and season with salt. The relish can be transferred to sterilized jars (see pages 134–35), if desired.

GREEN CHILLI RELISH

3 tbsp olive oil
250g (8oz) white or yellow onions, finely chopped
6 garlic cloves, chopped
500g (1lb) jalapeño or serrano chillies, roasted, peeled and deseeded (see page 96), finely chopped
1 tbsp dried oregano
250ml (8fl oz) white wine vinegar, cider vinegar or distilled vinegar
250ml (8fl oz) water
1 scant tbsp salt
1 tbsp flour mixed with 2 tbsp light oil

This is a superb fiery-hot South American chilli relish. It is used to flavour soups, salsas or mayonnaise, or to top hamburgers, grilled chicken or other meat.

Makes 750g (1½lb)

Shelf-life: 3 weeks in the refrigerator; 6 months in sealed jars

1 Heat the oil in a pan, add the onions and garlic and fry gently for about 5 minutes, or until the onions are translucent. Add the chillies, oregano, vinegar, water and salt and bring to the boil. Reduce the heat and simmer for about 20 minutes. If a smooth relish is preferred, process in a food processor, then return the mixture to the pan.

2 Add the flour and oil mixture and whisk well. Bring to the boil and cook for 5–8 minutes, whisking frequently, until the relish has thickened. The relish can be bottled (see pages 134–35), if desired.

HARISSA

Here is the recipe for this famous, fiercely hot Moroccan chilli sauce. You may like to tame the hotness by adding a little tomato paste or Tomato Purée (see page 43). About a tablespoon of dry-roasted cumin seeds can be added too.

Makes 500g (1lb)

Shelf-life: 3 months in the refrigerator; 1 year in sealed jars (make sure the surface of the paste is covered by a thin layer of oil)

See page 15 for illustration

500g (1lb) dried red chillies, stems removed

100g (3½oz) garlic

1 tbsp coriander seeds, dry-roasted (see page 78) and ground

150ml (¼ pint) olive oil

1½ tbsp salt

1 Put the chillies in a bowl, add enough hot water to cover them and leave to stand for 15–20 minutes until soft.

2 Drain the chillies and place in a food processor with about 125ml (4fl oz) of the soaking water. Whizz to a paste, add the garlic, coriander seeds, oil and salt and process. The harissa can be used immediately but can also be packed into sterilized jars (see pages 134–35).

FRUITY CHILLI RELISH

A deliciously hot relish, perfect with cold chicken, meat or mature cheeses; it can also be spread thickly over grilled lamb chops and caramelized under a hot grill.

Makes 900g (1lb 13oz)

Shelf-life: 3 months in the refrigerator; 1 year in sealed jars

500g (1lb) mangoes, peeled, stoned and coarsely chopped

2 large dessert apples, peeled, cored and coarsely chopped

2 onions, chopped

200g (7oz) red chillies, deseeded and chopped

200g (7oz) caster sugar

250ml (8fl oz) cider vinegar or wine vinegar

1 large bunch of fresh coriander, chopped

salt

1 Place the mangoes, apples, onions and chillies in a food processor and process until finely chopped but not puréed.

2 Transfer the chopped ingredients to a large pan and add the sugar. Cook over high heat for 8–10 minutes, or until most of the liquid has evaporated and the sugar is a pale caramel colour.

3 Mix in the vinegar and coriander and boil for 4–5 minutes, until the mixture is the consistency of jam. Season with salt to taste; bottle in sterilized jars (see pages 134–35), if desired.

TWO-TOMATO RELISH

1kg (2lb) cherry tomatoes

200g (7oz) sun-dried tomatoes in oil, chopped, oil reserved and extra olive oil added, if necessary, to make it up to 150ml (¼ pint)

150g (10oz) onions, chopped

6 garlic cloves, coarsely chopped

3 tbsp chopped fresh thyme

1–2 red chillies, deseeded and finely chopped

strained juice of 2 lemons

1–2 tbsp dark brown sugar (optional)

salt

Put all the ingredients in a deep roasting pan and roast in an oven preheated to 230°C/450°F/ Gas Mark 8 for about 45 minutes–1 hour, or until most of the liquid has evaporated. Store in sterilized jars (see pages 134–35), if desired.

Sun-dried tomatoes give a sunny Mediterranean flavour to this piquant relish.

Makes 600g (1lb 3½oz)

Shelf-life: 3 weeks in the refrigerator; 6 months in sealed jars

See page 17 for illustration

EXOTIC FRUIT RELISH

250g (8oz) palm or unrefined sugar

90ml (3fl oz) rice or white wine vinegar

1 small pineapple, peeled and finely chopped

5cm (2 inches) fresh ginger, finely shredded

3–4 red chillies, deseeded and finely chopped

6 garlic cloves, chopped

5 kaffir lime leaves

1 small bunch of fresh coriander, chopped

2–3 tbsp Thai fish sauce (*nam pla*)

1 Put the sugar and vinegar in a pan and boil until the sugar has dissolved and begun to caramelize.

2 Carefully tip (hot steam will be created) all the remaining ingredients except the fish sauce into the caramelized mixture and mix well.

3 Bring to the boil, add the fish sauce and cook for 5 minutes, or until the relish is thick and jam-like. Bottle in sterilized jars (see pages 134–35), if desired.

This is a superbly fragrant relish inspired by the flavours of Southeast Asian cooking. Serve this with chicken, fish or seafood. You could substitute mango or papaya for the pineapple.

Makes 500g (1lb)

Shelf-life: 3 months in the refrigerator; 1 year in sealed jars

See page 13 for illustration

RAITAS & SAMBALS

A LARGE FAMILY OF YOGURT-BASED SALADS, raitas are served as cooling accompaniments to hot curries or to add moisture to dry dishes. For a light, fresh summer main course, pour chilled raita over rice or burghul pilaff.

Sambals are a range of fresh salads and relishes that originated in Southeast Asia but were developed by the Cape Malays in South Africa. Serve them with grilled meat, curries or rice pilaffs.

ONION RAITA

This is a fresh, crunchy raita to be served with hot curries.

Shelf-life: 1 day in the refrigerator

4 onions, halved and thinly sliced
1 tbsp caster sugar, or crushed jaggery
250ml (8fl oz) yogurt
strained juice of 1/2 lemon
1 tsp nigella seeds, dry-roasted (see page 78)
1/4 tsp chilli powder or finely chopped fresh chilli (optional)
4 tbsp chopped fresh mint or coriander
salt and freshly ground black pepper

1 Place the onions in a colander, sprinkle over the sugar or jaggery and set aside to drain for about 1 hour. Squeeze out any excess liquid with your hands.

2 Mix the onions with the rest of the ingredients in a bowl and chill for at least 1 hour before serving.

TOMATO RAITA

Serve this with hot curries or as a cool dip with poppadoms. For a cucumber raita, substitute the same quantity of chopped cucumber and use dry-roasted fennel seeds instead of cumin seeds.

Shelf-life: 1 day in the refrigerator

See page 17 for illustration

350g (11½oz) plum or other fleshy tomatoes, peeled, deseeded (see page 43) and chopped
1 bunch of spring onions, chopped
250ml (8fl oz) yogurt
strained juice of 2 limes or 1 large lemon
a few gratings of lime or lemon zest
1/4 tsp chilli powder or 1 small chilli, chopped
1 tsp cumin seeds, dry-roasted (see page 78)
4 tbsp chopped fresh mint or coriander
salt

Mix all the ingredients together in a bowl. Chill for at least 1 hour before serving.

QUINCE SAMBAL

400g (13oz) ripe quinces, peeled and coarsely grated
2 tsp salt
5cm (2 inches) fresh ginger, finely grated
1–2 green chillies, deseeded and chopped
strained juice of 2 lemons
a few gratings of lemon zest

I like to serve this deliciously fragrant, autumnal sambal with grilled fish or curry.

Shelf-life: 3 days in the refrigerator

1 Put the quinces in a colander and sprinkle over the salt. Leave to drain for about 1 hour. Squeeze out any excess liquid with your hands.

2 In a bowl mix the quinces with the remaining ingredients. Taste the mixture and add a little more salt if necessary, then set aside to marinate for 1 hour before serving.

VARIATION

CARROT SAMBAL
Substitute grated carrots for the quinces and 1 bunch of chopped spring onions for the ginger. Omit the lemon juice and zest and add 3 tablespoons white wine vinegar or cider vinegar.

CUCUMBER SAMBAL

500g (1lb) firm cucumbers, coarsely grated
1 small onion, finely grated
6 anchovy fillets in oil, drained, finely chopped
2 green or red chillies, deseeded and finely chopped
3 tbsp white wine vinegar

Originally this sambal was flavoured with fermented fish or shrimp paste (blatjang) but I find that salted anchovies make a very good substitute. Use firm-fleshed cucumbers.

Shelf-life: 3 days in the refrigerator

Combine all the ingredients in a bowl and chill for an hour or so before serving.

DIPS

THESE RECIPES ARE PREDOMINANTLY Mediterranean in origin. They can be served as part of a mezze – a collection of small raw or cooked dishes designed to whet the appetite – or eaten as a light snack with a glass of wine or an apéritif. Make sure the dips are well chilled. Accompany them with a selection of fresh leaves, such as chicory or lettuce, batons of raw vegetables, and toast, crisps or warm pitta bread.

SMOKY AUBERGINE DIP

The bland flavour of aubergine makes it an ideal base for dips. You can cook the aubergine in a very hot oven or under a hot grill, but for a good smoky flavour, roast directly on an open gas flame or barbecue. For a smooth dip, purée the aubergine in a food processor. I sometimes stir in 6 tablespoons of tahini – which adds a slightly nutty flavour – and a little extra lemon juice.

Shelf-life: 1 week in the refrigerator

| 2–3 large aubergines |
| 1 large white or red onion, or 1 bunch of spring onions, chopped |
| 2–3 garlic cloves, crushed |
| 4–6 tbsp virgin olive oil |
| strained juice of 1–2 lemons (to taste) |
| a few gratings of lemon zest |
| 1–2 red or green chillies, deseeded and finely chopped |
| 4–5 tbsp chopped fresh parsley, mint or sweet marjoram, or a combination of all 3 |
| salt |

1 Roast or grill the aubergines until the skin is charred and the flesh is soft, about 10–15 minutes. Make a deep gash in each aubergine, then place in a colander until cool enough to handle. Peel the aubergines under cold running water, removing as much of the charred skin as possible.

2 Chop the aubergine flesh coarsely and return to a clean colander. Sprinkle with 1 teaspoon of salt, then cover and leave to drain for at least 1 hour. (You can speed up this process by gently squeezing the water from the aubergine flesh with your hands.)

3 Place the flesh on a chopping board and chop with a large knife or a mezzaluna (double-handed herb chopper) until puréed but still textured. Transfer to a bowl and mix in the remaining ingredients. Chill well before serving.

VARIATIONS

PEPPER & AUBERGINE DIP
Add 3 roasted and peeled (see page 96) red or mixed colour peppers to the finished aubergine dip.

FETA & AUBERGINE DIP
Stir in 200g (7oz) crumbled feta cheese and 100g (3½oz) peeled, deseeded (see page 43) and chopped tomatoes.

YOGURT, GARLIC & LEMON DIP

A fragrant, low-calorie dip that is especially good with seafood or vegetables. If sweet paprika is not available, use any other sweet pimiento powder.

Shelf-life: 1 day in the refrigerator

| 300ml (½ pint) full-fat or skimmed Greek-style yogurt |
| 1 pickled lemon, finely chopped |
| 1 garlic clove, crushed |
| 2 tbsp olive oil |
| 1–2 red chillies, finely chopped |
| 2 tsp sweet paprika |
| 3 tbsp chopped fresh dill or mint |
| salt |

Mix all the ingredients together in a bowl and chill well before serving.

VARIATION

SIMPLE YOGURT DIP
For a simple and versatile yogurt dip, substitute the juice of 1 lemon and a few gratings of lemon zest for the pickled lemon and fresh mint, parsley or coriander for the dill. Omit the chillies and paprika and add 3 tablespoons of either capers, pitted olives, anchovies, sun-dried tomatoes or gherkins. Season with salt and pepper.

BEAN DIP

This is a delicious, slightly nutty-flavoured dip to serve with raw vegetables, crisps, tortilla chips or warmed pitta bread.

Shelf-life: *3 days in the refrigerator*

200g (7oz) haricot beans

4 tbsp extra-virgin olive oil

1 large onion, finely chopped

strained juice of 1 large lemon

3 tbsp chopped fresh flat-leaf parsley or mint

salt and freshly ground black pepper

1 Soak the beans overnight in enough cold water to cover them. Drain, then boil them in plenty of water until soft, about 1 hour. Drain well, reserving the cooking liquid.

2 Place the beans in a food processor and process to a smooth purée with a little of the cooking liquid.

3 Heat the oil in a frying pan, add the onion and fry until crisp and golden brown, about 10–15 minutes.

4 Transfer the bean purée to a bowl, add the fried onion and mix in the rest of the ingredients. Add a little more cooking liquid if the mixture is too thick. Serve warm or at room temperature.

PEPPER DIP

For smoother results, make this dip in a food processor. I sometimes roast and peel the peppers (see page 96), which gives the dip a more pronounced flavour.

Shelf-life: *3 days in the refrigerator*

250g (8oz) fromage frais, or curd cheese diluted with a little milk or yogurt

3 peppers, preferably red, yellow and green, cored, deseeded and finely chopped

1–2 red or green chillies, deseeded and finely chopped (optional)

4–5 spring onions, finely chopped

1 tsp caraway seeds, coarsely ground

3 tbsp chopped fresh dill

strained juice of 1 lemon, or to taste

salt and freshly ground black pepper

Mix all the ingredients together in a bowl or food processor and refrigerate for at least 2 hours before serving.

TARAMASALATA

150g (5oz) smoked cod roe, or 125g (4oz) tarama paste

1 small onion, finely grated

150g (5oz) crustless white bread, soaked in water and squeezed dry

strained juice of 1 lemon, or more to taste

grated zest of ½ lemon (optional)

1 small garlic clove, crushed (optional)

250–300ml (8–10fl oz) extra-virgin olive oil, or a mixture of olive and groundnut oil

1 If using cod roe, put it in a bowl, pour over boiling water to cover and soak for 5 minutes. Drain, refresh with cold water, then peel off and discard the membrane.

2 Put the cod roe or tarama paste, onion, bread, lemon juice and zest and garlic, if using, in a food processor and process until smooth. With the machine running, add the oil in a thin, steady stream; process until the consistency of mayonnaise.

Smooth and delicately pink, this famous Greek dip can be diluted with a little lemon juice, water or milk and served as a piquant sauce with grilled fish or seafood. Smoked cod roe is available from any good fishmonger.

Shelf-life: *3 days in the refrigerator*

SOURED CREAM & SAFFRON DIP

30g (1oz) butter or olive oil

100g (3½oz) shallots, finely chopped

125ml (4fl oz) dry white wine

¼ tsp saffron strands, soaked in 2 tbsp warm water or white wine

250ml (8fl oz) soured cream or crème fraîche

1–2 tbsp lemon juice, or to taste

salt

With a delicate golden colour, this dip goes particularly well with prawns or raw vegetables. For a spicier dip, use 1–2 tablespoons of curry powder instead of the saffron.

Shelf-life: *3 days in the refrigerator*

1 Heat the butter or olive oil in a small pan, add the shallots and fry until golden. Add the wine and the saffron mixture and bring to the boil. Reduce the heat and simmer until most of the liquid has evaporated, 10 minutes or so. Remove from the heat and allow to cool.

2 In a bowl, mix the cooled shallot mixture with the remaining ingredients. Chill for at least 1 hour before serving.

MARINADES & SPICE PASTES

THESE HERB- AND SPICE-PACKED MARINADES AND PASTES ARE A CONVENIENT WAY TO INTRODUCE

FLAVOUR, TENDERIZE TOUGH CUTS OF MEAT AND TURN SIMPLE FOODS INTO SPECIAL TREATS WITH THE

MINIMUM OF FUSS. MARINATING TIME IS DICTATED BY THE THICKNESS OF THE FOOD BEING MARINATED –

THE THICKER IT IS, THE LONGER YOU WILL NEED TO LEAVE IT FOR THE FLAVOURS TO PENETRATE. DURING

THE MARINATING PERIOD, COVER THE FOOD TO PROTECT IT FROM DUST AND INSECTS AND, WHENEVER

POSSIBLE, MARINATE IN THE REFRIGERATOR. TURN THE FOOD IN THE MARINADE FROM TIME TO TIME TO

ENSURE IT IS EVENLY AND THOROUGHLY COATED.

LAVENDER LAMB MARINADE

I have tried many versions of this aromatic marinade, changing the herbs according to their availability. Any fragrant herb can be used but my favourite is lavender – both the leaves and flowering heads. This is a delicious marinade for lamb kebabs.

Enough for 1kg (2lb) lamb

Marinating time:
5–24 hours

4–5 garlic cloves

1 small onion, roughly chopped

150ml (¼ pint) olive oil

juice and grated zest of 1 large lemon
(zest optional)

about 100g (3½ oz) coarsely chopped or bruised fresh herbs of your choice, such as lavender leaves and flowering heads, wild or garden thyme, rosemary, wild marjoram

salt and coarsely ground black pepper

1 Place the garlic and onion in a food processor and process to a smooth paste. Add the olive oil, lemon juice and zest, if using, and process. Add the herbs and salt and pepper.

2 Pour the marinade over the meat, cover and marinate in the refrigerator.

MEDITERRANEAN FISH ▷ MARINADE

juice of 1–2 lemons

grated zest of 1 lemon

6 tbsp good olive oil

2 garlic cloves, crushed

1 tsp black peppercorns, crushed

1 tsp fennel seeds, dry-roasted
(see page 78) and crushed

1 small bunch of fresh parsley, dill or wild fennel tops, finely chopped

salt

This is especially delicious as a marinade for whole fish such as bass or tuna or grey or red mullet. It is also good with oily fish such as mackerel and sardines.

Enough for 1kg (2lb) fish

Marinating time:
2–4 hours

See page 11 for illustration

Mix all the ingredients together in a bowl. Make 3 slashes on each side of the fish, then pour the marinade over the fish in a shallow dish. Cover and leave to marinate in the refrigerator before either grilling, baking or frying the fish.

OPPOSITE: SALMON FILLETS IN MEDITERRANEAN FISH MARINADE

CIDER & HERB MARINADE

This is wonderful for pork chops or large pieces of pork, and also for chicken, duck or rabbit. If the marinade doesn't cover the meat, turn it from time to time to coat it thoroughly.

Enough for 2–3kg (4–6lb) meat

Marinating time: 12 hours; 3 days for larger pieces of meat

1 litre (1¾ pints) cider
100ml (3½fl oz) cider vinegar
3 tbsp honey or sugar
2 tart apples, chopped or grated
2 celery stalks, chopped
1 small bunch of fresh thyme, bruised
6–8 fresh sage leaves, bruised
2 bay leaves
1 tbsp coriander seeds, crushed
½ tsp cloves, crushed
1 tsp black peppercorns, crushed

Mix all the ingredients together, pour them over your chosen meat in a shallow dish and leave to marinate in the refrigerator.

TRADITIONAL BARBECUE SAUCE

One of the cornerstones of North American barbecue culture, this versatile sauce is used to marinate beef, chicken, ribs or pork. It is good for basting meats while cooking and can also be served as a side sauce for many grilled and barbecued dishes.

Enough for about 2kg (4lb) meat

Marinating time: 2–24 hours

Shelf-life: 6 months in sealed bottles

4 tbsp groundnut or sesame oil
1 large onion, finely chopped
4 garlic cloves, finely chopped
1 tbsp chilli powder
500ml (17fl oz) tomato ketchup
250ml (8fl oz) cider vinegar
4 tbsp lemon juice
4 tbsp Worcestershire sauce
5 tbsp soft dark brown sugar
1 tbsp celery seeds, crushed

1 Heat the oil in a pan, add the onion and garlic and fry gently until the onion is golden and soft.

2 Add the rest of the ingredients, bring to the boil, then reduce the heat and simmer for 30 minutes. Set aside to cool a little, then pour over meat. Leave to cool completely, then cover and marinate in the refrigerator. The sauce can be bottled, if desired (see pages 134–35).

TANDOORI MARINADE

6 garlic cloves
5cm (2 inches) fresh ginger
250ml (8fl oz) plain yogurt
juice of 2 limes or 1 lemon
grated zest of ½ lime
2 tbsp ground coriander
1 tbsp sweet paprika
1 tbsp ground cumin
1 tbsp ground turmeric
1–2 tsp chilli powder
½ tsp ground cardamom
1 tbsp salt

Traditionally tandoori marinade is bright red but this effect is achieved with artificial colouring. I prefer tandoori to be the natural colour of the aromatic spices it contains.

Enough for about 1–1.5kg (2–3lb) skinless chicken pieces or lamb chops

Marinating time: 12–24 hours

See page 19 for illustration

1 Place the garlic and ginger in a spice mill or food processor and process to a smooth purée. Add the rest of the ingredients and process until well mixed.

2 Pour over skinned chicken pieces or lamb chops in a shallow dish, cover and marinate in the refrigerator. Bake in a clay tandoor or hot oven; alternatively, grill or barbecue.

BARBECUE SAUCE WITH COCOA

4 tbsp cocoa powder
200ml (7fl oz) red wine vinegar
200g (7oz) tomato purée
8 tbsp honey or 100g (3½oz) soft dark brown sugar
2 tbsp olive oil
10 garlic cloves, crushed
3–4 fresh red chillies, finely chopped, or chilli powder to taste (optional)
1 tbsp dried oregano (optional)
2 tbsp soy sauce
salt to taste

Cocoa powder is an unusual addition to this classic sauce, but it gives an intensity of flavour and a wonderful dark colour. Use it to marinate, as a baste for barbecueing or simply as a dipping sauce for barbecued meat or vegetables.

Enough for 2kg (4lb) meat

Marinating time: 2–24 hours

Shelf-life: 6 months in sealed bottles

Dissolve the cocoa powder in a little of the vinegar and place in a pan with the rest of the ingredients. Bring to the boil, then reduce the heat and simmer, stirring, for 20 minutes. Use to marinate meat in the refrigerator, or bottle (see pages 134–35).

ORANGE & GINGER SAUCE ▷

A tangy, slightly sharp-tasting sauce that goes very well with pork, duck and chicken. It can be used as a marinade or for basting meat while cooking, or even as a side sauce. This is really delicious with pork or chicken kebabs.

Enough for 2kg (4lb) meat

Marinating time:
4–24 hours for pork;
3–4 hours for chicken;
4–5 hours for duck

Shelf-life: 6 months in sealed bottles

500ml (17fl oz) orange juice
grated zest of 1 orange
4 tbsp tomato purée
100ml (3½fl oz) tomato ketchup
75ml (2½fl oz) cider vinegar or white wine vinegar
4 tbsp olive oil
3 tbsp dark soy sauce
4 tbsp molasses
4 garlic cloves, crushed or processed to a smooth paste
1 small onion, finely grated or processed to a smooth paste
5cm (2 inches) fresh ginger, finely grated or processed to a smooth paste
1–2 fresh, hot red chillies, deseeded and finely chopped, or chilli powder to taste
1 tsp arrowroot or cornflour, dissolved in 2 tbsp vinegar (optional)
salt

Put the orange juice in a pan and bring to the boil, skimming any scum from the surface. Boil until reduced by half, then add all the rest of the ingredients except the arrowroot or cornflour, if using, and simmer for 20 minutes. If the sauce is too thin, add the arrowroot or cornflour and boil until it thickens. Use for marinating or basting, or bottle (see pages 134–35).

BEER MARINADE

Use this to marinate joints of beef, wild boar or venison.

Enough for a 1–2kg (2–4lb) joint

Marinating time:
12 hours – 2 days

750ml (1¼ pints) good, flavoursome ale or beer
5 tbsp brown sugar such as muscovado
4 tbsp malt vinegar
1 tbsp allspice berries, crushed
1 small bunch of fresh thyme, chopped
2–3 bay leaves

Mix all the ingredients together in a shallow dish large enough to hold the joint. Add the meat, cover and leave to marinate in the refrigerator, then roast as normal.

RIGHT: ORANGE & GINGER SAUCE ON A PORK KEBAB

◁ CEVICHE

strained juice of 3 limes
grated zest of 1 lime
100g (3½ oz) plum or other fleshy tomato, peeled, deseeded (see page 43) and finely chopped
1 small red or sweet white onion, finely chopped
1–3 green or red chillies, deseeded and finely chopped
3 tbsp light olive or groundnut oil
1–2 fresh lime or lemon leaves, finely shredded (optional)
2 tsp salt
3 tbsp chopped fresh coriander or flat-leaf parsley

A delicious, light and tangy marinade for raw fish salad. The fresh lime juice 'cooks' the fish. Use very fresh fish steaks such as tuna, swordfish, barramundi or even salmon.

Enough for 500g (1lb) skinless fish steaks, cut into cubes

Marinating time: 2–24 hours

Shelf-life: 24 hours in the refrigerator

Mix all the ingredients except the coriander or parsley together, then pour over the cubed fish in a small bowl. Cover and leave to marinate in the refrigerator. Stir in the coriander or parsley just before serving.

TZARAMELO

strained juice of 2 lemons
grated zest of ½ lemon
2 plum tomatoes, peeled, deseeded (see page 43) and finely chopped
2 garlic cloves, finely chopped
1 green pepper, deseeded and finely chopped
1–2 red or green chillies, finely chopped, or chilli powder to taste (optional)
1 small red or white onion, finely chopped
1 small bunch of fresh dill, snipped
salt and freshly ground black pepper

This Mediterranean marinade is delicious with fried fish such as red mullet but is also good with chicken. It should be poured over hot fish or meat.

Enough for 1.5–2kg (3–4lb) fish or chicken

Marinating time: 5–10 minutes, turning the fish or meat frequently to ensure it is evenly coated

Mix all the ingredients together in a bowl. Pour the marinade over hot grilled or fried fish or chicken and leave to marinate before serving.

LEFT: SUCCULENT CUBES OF SWORDFISH IN A ZESTY CEVICHE

ORIENTAL SOY MARINADE

Adapt this recipe to your own taste by adding flavourings such as spring onions, lemongrass, shallots and different herbs and spices. Use it to marinate chicken pieces, fatty cuts of meat or cubed tofu.

Enough to marinate 500g (1lb) chicken pieces, fatty cuts of meat and tofu

Marinating time: *4 hours*

6 tbsp dark soy sauce
2 tbsp palm or soft dark brown sugar
3 star anise, crushed
2 garlic cloves, crushed
5cm (2 inches) fresh ginger, chopped (optional)
1–2 fresh chillies, chopped (optional)

Mix all the ingredients together and pour over meat or cubed tofu in a shallow dish. Cover and marinate in the refrigerator.

LEMON & CHILLI MARINADE

This marinade should be poured over cooked fish, such as bass, snapper or Atlantic fish steaks. It is also delicious with chicken.

Enough for 1–1.5kg (2–3lb) fish or chicken

Marinating time: *5–10 minutes, turning the fish or chicken from time to time to ensure it is evenly coated*

juice of 1 large lemon and grated zest of ½
3 tbsp water
3 garlic cloves, crushed
3 tbsp fruity olive oil
1 tbsp (or more to taste) Harissa (see page 103) or chopped fresh chilli
2 tsp sweet paprika
½ large bunch of fresh parsley, chopped
salt

Mix all the ingredients together in a bowl; pour over hot fish or chicken to marinate.

APRICOT & HERB MARINADE

This is delicious on pork chops or steaks; it should be poured over while the meat is still hot and left to marinate only briefly.

Enough for 1kg (2lb) pork chops or steaks

Marinating time: *5–10 minutes, turning the meat from time to time to ensure it is evenly coated*

4 tbsp apricot jam
100ml (3½fl oz) white wine or dry cider
4–5 fresh sage leaves, chopped, or 1–2 tbsp chopped fresh rosemary
3 tbsp rum
salt and freshly ground black pepper

Place the jam and wine or cider in a pan and bring to the boil. Reduce the heat and simmer, stirring, for 1–2 minutes to melt the jam. Remove from the heat and add the remaining ingredients, then pour the marinade over grilled or fried pork chops or steaks and leave to marinate.

CHIMICHURRI

5 garlic cloves, crushed
1–2 or more red jalapeño or Anaheim chillies, deseeded and finely chopped
5 tbsp red wine vinegar
125ml (4fl oz) olive oil
4 tbsp finely chopped fresh oregano or 1 tbsp dried oregano
1 bunch of fresh coriander or flat-leaf parsley, finely chopped
salt

A hot and spicy Mexican marinade for pork or beef that can also be used as a basting sauce or a dip. You can use a food processor or a blender to purée the ingredients instead of chopping them by hand.

Enough for 2kg (4lb) meat

Marinating time: *2–12 hours*

Combine all the ingredients in a bowl, add the meat, coating it in the mixture, and leave to marinate in the refrigerator.

SOUTH AFRICAN SOSATIE

50ml (2fl oz) groundnut or light olive oil
500g (1lb) onions, thinly sliced
5cm (2 inches) fresh ginger, chopped
3 garlic cloves, chopped
1–2 tbsp curry powder
100g (3½oz) tamarind pulp, soaked in 300ml (½ pint) hot water or red wine vinegar, sieved (see page 124)
1–2 lemon, orange or kaffir lime leaves, finely shredded
salt

Mildly curry-flavoured, this marinade is traditionally used with mutton but is also good with lamb, beef or chicken. For a pleasant fruity edge, add 1–2 tablespoons of apricot chutney with the tamarind water.

Enough for 1kg (2lb) meat

Marinating time: *12 hours*

See page 13 for illustration

1 Heat the oil in a large frying pan, add the onions and fry for 8–10 minutes, or until lightly browned. Add the rest of the ingredients and bring to the boil, then remove from the heat and set aside to cool.

2 Pour the cooled marinade over the meat and leave to marinate in the refrigerator for 12 hours, then lift the meat out and barbecue, using a little of the marinade for basting.

3 Place the remaining marinade in a pan, bring to the boil and simmer gently until most of the liquid has evaporated. Serve the reduced onion mixture on top of the barbecued meat.

HERB PASTE FOR FISH

This gives a fresh, tangy flavour to baked sea bass, salmon, snapper or any other large fish; it also keeps the fish wonderfully moist.

Enough for a 1–1.5kg (2–3lb) fish

Marinating time:
30 minutes – 1 hour

60g (2oz) butter
2 tbsp olive oil
¼ tsp fennel seeds
150g (5oz) shallots, or 1 onion, finely chopped
2.5cm (1 inch) fresh ginger, finely chopped
1 x 60g (2oz) tin of anchovies, drained and chopped
1 small bunch of fresh dill, finely chopped
1 small bunch of fresh parsley, finely chopped
1 tbsp capers, drained and rinsed
juice and grated zest of ½ lemon
3 tbsp breadcrumbs

1 Heat the butter and olive oil in a frying pan, add the fennel seeds and fry gently for a few minutes. Add the shallots or onion and the ginger and fry until they start to change colour, about 5–8 minutes. Remove from the heat and stir in the rest of the ingredients.

2 Stuff some of the paste into the belly of the fish and pile the rest over it in an ovenproof baking dish. Marinate in the refrigerator, then bake as normal.

PASTE FOR COOKED MEATS

A superb way of adding flavour to cold cooked meat. I use it for boiled bacon, fatty joints of pork, brisket or cooked or cured turkey breast.

Enough for 1–1.5kg (2–3lb) meat

Marinating time: at least 2 days

Shelf-life: 1 week in the refrigerator

100g (3½oz) garlic, peeled
4 tbsp sweet Hungarian paprika
1–2 tsp hot Hungarian paprika or chilli powder
1 tbsp salt
2 tbsp caraway seeds, finely ground
1 tbsp freshly ground black pepper
2 tbsp olive oil

1 Process the garlic to a purée in a food processor, then mix with all the remaining ingredients.

2 Spread a thick coating of the paste all over the cooked meat, then leave to marinate in an airtight container in the refrigerator. Cut into thin slices to serve.

PAPAYA MARINATING PASTE

1 small (100–150g/3½–5oz) unripe papaya, peeled, halved, deseeded and coarsely chopped
the papaya seeds, crushed to a paste
100ml (3½fl oz) coconut milk or water
5cm (2 inches) fresh ginger, chopped
2 lemongrass stalks, hard outer layers removed, chopped
1–2 fresh chillies, or chilli powder to taste
salt

Unripe green papayas contain a large amount of papain, an enzyme that tenderizes meat. This puréed papaya paste works very well on tough cuts of meat such as beef or mutton. Fresh pineapple can be used instead of the papaya.

Enough for 1kg (2lb) meat

Marinating time:
up to 12 hours

Place all the ingredients in a food processor and process to a smooth paste. Cover the meat in the paste and marinate in the refrigerator.

JAMAICAN JERK PASTE

1 onion, peeled and quartered
6 garlic cloves
250g (8oz) Habañero chillies, deseeded
100g (3½oz) fresh ginger, peeled
1 small bunch of fresh flat-leaf parsley
1 bunch of spring onions
4 tbsp ground allspice
60g (2oz) fresh thyme, chopped, or 2 tbsp dried thyme
1 tsp ground cloves
2–3 tbsp dark soy sauce
strained juice of 3 limes

Habanero chillies are dangerously hot and I advise actually wearing gloves when handling them. For milder results, use a milder chilli such as Jalapeño for the Habanera chillies.

Enough for 1–1.5kg (2–3lb) meat

Marinating time:
12–24 hours

Shelf-life: 1 week in the refrigerator; 3 months in the freezer; 6 months in sealed jars (see pages 134–35)

Purée the first 6 ingredients in a food processor, then add the remaining ingredients and process to mix. Pour the mixture over the meat in a shallow dish and marinate in the refrigerator.

NORTH AFRICAN SPICE PASTE

A wonderfully fragrant paste that is very good with grilled or barbecued chicken, or lamb or mutton chops. Fragrant and strongly flavoured, preserved lemons are popular in North African cooking – look for them in North African and Middle Eastern grocers.

Enough for about 1.5–2kg (3–4lb) meat

Marinating time:
12–24 hours

8 garlic cloves, crushed

2 preserved lemons with pips removed, finely chopped

2.5cm (1 inch) fresh ginger, chopped

2 tsp salt

½ tsp ground mace

¼ tsp cumin seeds, dry-roasted (see page 78) and ground

¼ tsp powdered saffron or ½ tsp saffron strands, crushed

3 tbsp chopped fresh coriander

Place the garlic, preserved lemons and ginger in a spice mill or a food processor and process to a smooth purée. Add the rest of the ingredients and process. Massage the paste into the meat and leave to marinate in the refrigerator.

HERB RUB

Use herbs such as rosemary, thyme, sage and oregano and rub into lamb chops, chicken pieces or game steaks for delicious results.

Enough for about 1–1.5kg (2–3lb) meat

Marinating time:
4–24 hours

Shelf-life: 3 months in an airtight container (but use dried instead of fresh herbs and add the garlic just before use)

100g (3½oz) mixture of fresh herbs such as rosemary, thyme, sage and oregano, finely chopped, or 4 tbsp mixed dried herbs

4 garlic cloves, crushed

1 tbsp salt

grated zest of 1 lemon

1 tbsp coarsely ground black peppercorns

1 tbsp coarsely ground white peppercorns

1 tsp finely ground allspice

1 tbsp mustard powder

Combine all the ingredients in a shallow dish. Dip each piece of meat into the mixture so that it is well coated, then cover and marinate in the refrigerator before either frying, grilling or barbecuing.

TRADITIONAL RIB RUB

150g (5oz) dark soft brown sugar

2 tbsp salt

4 tbsp sweet paprika or other pimento powder

3 tbsp coarsely ground or crushed black peppercorns

2 tbsp mustard powder

2 tsp chilli powder

2 garlic cloves, crushed

Essential for barbecued or hot-smoked ribs, but also delicious with barbecued chicken.

Enough for 2kg (4lb) ribs or two 1.5kg (3lb) chickens

Marinating time:
24–48 hours

Shelf-life: up to 3 days in the refrigerator

Mix all the ingredients together. Massage the mixture into the meat, rubbing it into all the crevices. Cover and leave to marinate in the refrigerator.

INDIAN DRY RUB

4 tbsp gram (chickpea) flour

2 tbsp fennel seeds, dry-roasted (see page 78)

2 tbsp coriander seeds, dry-roasted (see page 78)

1 tbsp cumin seeds, dry-roasted (see page 78)

1 tsp cardamom pods, dry-roasted (see page 78)

1 tbsp freshly ground black pepper

2 tsp ground turmeric

½–1 tsp chilli powder

¼ tsp asafoetida (optional)

This fragrant and spicy rub is especially good with chicken or fish. The fennel, coriander seeds, cumin and cardamom pods can be dry-roasted together.

Enough for about 500g (1lb) meat or fish

Marinating time:
6–24 hours

Shelf-life: 3 months in an airtight container

1 Put all the ingredients in a spice mill or a blender and process to a fine powder.

2 Transfer the powder to a shallow dish, then dip the meat or fish into it so that it is evenly coated in the mixture. Cover and leave to marinate in the refrigerator, then either fry, grill or barbecue.

SIDE SAUCES

FRUITY, PIQUANT OR SPICY, SIDE SAUCES CAN ADD TANTALIZING INTEREST TO THE SIMPLEST MEAL. HERE IS A

COLLECTION OF MY FAVOURITES FROM ALL OVER THE WORLD. IF YOU HAVE TIME, PREPARE LARGER QUANTITIES

AND PACK INTO JARS — THEY MAKE EXCELLENT STORECUPBOARD STAND-BYS AS WELL AS ATTRACTIVE GIFTS.

APPLE SAUCE

This delicious sauce is the traditional accompaniment to roast pork; it is perfect with rösti potatoes and also makes a wonderful pancake filling. For extra richness, add 2–3 tablespoons of soured cream or crème fraîche.

Serves 6–8

Shelf-life: *1 week in the refrigerator; 6 months in a sealed jar (see pages 134–35)*

500g (1lb) cooking apples, such as Bramley, peeled, cored and roughly chopped

2–3 tbsp white or brown sugar or honey, or more to taste

1–2 tbsp white wine or water

3–4 cloves

5cm (2 inches) cinnamon stick

2–3 strips of lemon or orange zest

30g (1oz) butter

2–3 tbsp soured cream or crème fraîche (optional)

salt

1 Put the apples, sugar or honey and white wine or water in a pan. Add the cloves, cinnamon and lemon or orange zest and bring to the boil. Reduce the heat, then cover and cook gently until the apples are soft and beginning to disintegrate, about 10–15 minutes. Remove from the heat, fish out the cloves, cinnamon stick and lemon or orange zest and discard.

2 Transfer to a blender or food processor, or use a wooden spoon or an electric wand mixer to beat the mixture to a smooth purée. Return it to the heat, season with a little salt, then beat in the butter and soured cream or crème fraîche, if using.

CRANBERRY SAUCE

250g (8oz) fresh or frozen cranberries

juice and grated zest of 1 orange

100ml (3½fl oz) water

1 large cooking apple, such as Bramley, peeled, cored and coarsely grated

125g (4oz) light brown or molasses sugar

60ml (2fl oz) Grand Marnier, or any other orange liqueur

1 tsp coriander seeds, dry-roasted (see page 78) and coarsely crushed

coarsely ground black pepper

This fragrant, bitter-sweet sauce is a must for roast turkey but also goes very well with cold roast pork and lamb.

Serves 6–8

Shelf-life: *1 week in the refrigerator; 6 months in a sealed jar (see pages 134–35)*

1 Put the cranberries, orange juice and zest, water, apple and sugar in a pan and bring slowly to the boil. Reduce the heat and simmer gently until the apple and cranberries are soft and beginning to disintegrate, about 12–15 minutes.

2 Remove from the heat and stir in the Grand Marnier and coriander seeds, then season with black pepper. Set aside to cool before serving.

OPPOSITE: CRANBERRY SAUCE SIMMERING IN THE EARLY STAGES OF COOKING

GOOSEBERRY SAUCE

Tart, refreshing and pale green in colour, this sauce is especially good with oily fish such as mackerel, herring or sardines. I also serve it with pork, goose and duck.

Serves 6–8

Shelf-life: 1 week in the refrigerator; 6 months in a sealed jar (see pages 134–35)

500g (1lb) gooseberries, topped and tailed
3 tbsp water
1–2 tbsp sugar, or more to taste
30g (1oz) butter
a pinch of nutmeg (optional)
salt

1 Put the gooseberries, water and sugar in a pan, bring to the boil and simmer until tender and mushy, about 15 minutes. Process to a smooth purée in a food processor or blender; alternatively, pass through a sieve.

2 Return the mixture to a clean pan and bring to the boil, then add the butter, stirring until it has melted and been mixed in. Season with the nutmeg, if using, and salt.

VARIATION

PLUM OR CHERRY SAUCE *See page 21 for illustration*
Both sauces make a refreshing accompaniment to gammon. Follow the recipe above but substitute 500g (1lb) stoned plums, such as Victoria or Switzen, or cherries for the gooseberries and use 100ml (3½fl oz) white wine or water. Simmer for about 20 minutes, until tender and mushy, then purée in a food processor or blender until smooth. Finish by stirring in a pinch of cinnamon.

FRESH BERRY SAUCE

This takes no time at all to prepare and makes a delightful, fruity yet spicy accompaniment to fish or chicken.

Serves 6–8

Shelf-life: 3 days in the refrigerator

300g (10oz) fresh berries, such as raspberries, blackberries, strawberries or blueberries, coarsely chopped or roughly mashed
4 spring onions, finely chopped
1 tsp green peppercorns in brine, coarsely chopped
2 tbsp raspberry or other berry-flavoured vinegar
1–2 tbsp sugar, or to taste
1–2 tbsp chopped fresh tarragon or chervil
salt

Mix all the ingredients together in a bowl and set aside to marinate for at least 1 hour before serving.

CUMBERLAND SAUCE

very thinly pared zest of 1 orange, cut into fine julienne
very thinly pared zest of 1 lemon, cut into fine julienne
250g (8oz) redcurrant jelly
4 tbsp port
strained juice of 1 orange
strained juice of 1 lemon
50g (1¾oz) shallots, finely chopped (optional)
a pinch of ground ginger
a pinch of cayenne pepper

1 Blanch the orange and lemon zest in boiling water for 1 minute, then drain, refresh in cold water and drain again well.

2 In a small pan, melt the jelly over a gentle heat, then add the port and simmer for about 3 minutes. Remove from the heat and stir in the blanched zest, the orange and lemon juice, the shallots, if using, and the ginger and cayenne pepper. Set aside to cool before serving.

VARIATION

CHERRY CUMBERLAND SAUCE
This is excellent with duck, pork or venison. Follow the recipe above from step 2, omitting the orange and lemon zest and juice. Instead, add 250g (8oz) chopped fresh or tinned sour cherries to the redcurrant jelly as it is heated, and stir in 1 teaspoon made English mustard with the shallots, if using, and the ginger and cayenne pepper.

MINT SAUCE

100–150g (3½–5oz) fresh mint, leaves only
1 tbsp caster sugar
3–4 tbsp white or red wine vinegar

Put the mint leaves on a chopping board, sprinkle over the sugar and chop finely. Alternatively, process the mint and sugar in a food processor until finely chopped but not puréed. Transfer the chopped mint to a small bowl and mix with the vinegar.

One of the great British sauces, this is traditionally served with cold ham, pork or lamb. I like to add chopped raw shallots (an 18th-century idea), which give a marvellous texture and flavour.

Serves 6–8

Shelf-life: 1 week in the refrigerator (without the shallots)

Mint sauce made with fresh garden mint is easy to prepare and far superior to the sickly-sweet commercial alternative. It complements lamb or mutton.

Serves 6–8

Shelf-life: 1 week in the refrigerator; 6 months in a sealed jar (see pages 134–35)

BREAD SAUCE

This is an adaptation of a 17th-century recipe, although bread sauce is medieval in origin. Mild and delicately flavoured, it is traditionally served with roast game, poultry or pork. Bread sauce should be porridge-like in consistency, but if you prefer a thinner sauce, dilute it with a little milk or cream. For a more intense flavour, don't discard the onion used to flavour the milk – process it or pass it through a sieve and add it to the sauce at the end.

Serves 6–8

Shelf-life: *1 week in the refrigerator*

1 small onion, peeled and quartered

4 cloves

1 small blade of mace

1 bay leaf

350ml (12fl oz) milk

90g (3oz) fresh white breadcrumbs

3 tbsp double cream

freshly ground nutmeg to taste

30g (1oz) butter

salt and freshly ground black pepper

1 Stud each of the onion quarters with a clove and add to the milk in a small pan along with the mace and bay leaf. Bring to the boil, then reduce the heat and simmer for about 20 minutes.

2 Strain into the top of a double boiler or into a bowl placed over a pan of just-simmering water, making sure the base of the bowl does not touch the water.

3 Sprinkle in the breadcrumbs and stir in the cream, then simmer until the sauce is smooth and thick, about 30 minutes.

4 Season with nutmeg and salt and pepper, then beat in the butter and serve hot.

HORSERADISH CREAM SAUCE

125g (4oz) fresh horseradish, peeled and finely grated, or prepared frozen or bottled horseradish

3 tbsp cider vinegar or white wine vinegar

1 tbsp caster sugar

100ml (3½fl oz) double cream

salt

Mix all the ingredients together in a bowl. The horseradish can be bottled in sterilized jars if desired (see pages 134–35). Fresh horseradish can be very potent – when you work with it, always make sure the room is well ventilated.

I love fresh horseradish sauce with its unique heat and head-clearing qualities. It is traditionally served with roast beef but I also serve it with cold meats, as a dip for vegetables and as a sandwich filling.

Serves 6–8

Shelf-life: *1 week in the refrigerator; 6 months in a sealed jar (see pages 134–35) but some of its potency is lost with keeping*

CHRAIN (HORSERADISH & BEETROOT SAUCE)

100g (3½oz) horseradish, peeled and finely grated, or prepared frozen or bottled horseradish

150g (5oz) beetroot, raw or cooked, peeled and finely grated

3 tbsp distilled vinegar or wine vinegar

1–2 tbsp caster sugar

salt

Mix all the ingredients together in a bowl. The sauce can be bottled in sterilized jars, if desired (see pages 134–35).

A Jewish version of horseradish sauce, chrain is traditionally served with fish. Beetroot lends it a vibrant purple colour and a sharper flavour.

Serves 6–8

Shelf-life: *3 weeks in the refrigerator; 6 months in a sealed jar (see pages 134–35) but some of its potency is lost with keeping*

CUMBERLAND SAUCE

MINT SAUCE

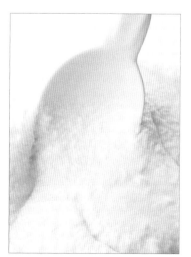
BREAD SAUCE

CHRAIN

PESTO ▷

A herb paste traditionally made from basil, pesto is usually served with pasta but can also be poured over fish or meat before or after grilling. Try it spread over crostini, too, or added to stews, sauces and soups for extra flavour. It is best made in a pestle and mortar, which gives it its characteristic texture and intense flavour.

Shelf-life: *1 week in the refrigerator (make sure there is a protective layer of oil over the pesto), although best eaten immediately*

2 large garlic cloves, halved and bashed with the flat side of a large knife
½ tsp coarse salt
60g (2oz) pine nuts, dry-roasted until golden brown (see page 78)
125g (4oz) fresh basil leaves
60g (2oz) Parmesan or Pecorino cheese, freshly grated
125ml (4fl oz) extra-virgin olive oil

BY HAND: (shown opposite)
1 Put the garlic and salt in a heavy mortar and work to a paste with the pestle.

2 Add the roasted pine nuts and continue pounding and mixing until smooth.

3 Start adding the basil a small handful at a time and pound and mix until smooth. Sprinkle in the cheese and mix well.

4 Slowly pour in the olive oil in a steady stream and mix until it has a paste-like consistency. Add a little more salt to taste, if necessary, and either serve immediately or transfer to a sterilized container (see pages 134–35).

MACHINE METHOD: put the garlic, salt, roasted pine nuts, basil and a few tablespoons of the oil in a food processor and process to a paste. Add the cheese and, with the machine running, slowly pour in the remaining oil in a thin, steady stream.

VARIATION

CORIANDER PESTO
This is a refreshing and piquant take on traditional pesto. Serve it as a dip for vegetables, savoury pastries or toasted pitta bread. It is delicious in sandwiches but can also be served in the same way as traditional pesto, with pasta or noodles. Like basil pesto, coriander pesto can be made with a pestle and mortar or in a food processor. Follow the recipe above but substitute 60g (2oz) dry-roasted pistachio nuts for the pine nuts, and instead of basil, use the same amount of coriander – stems and roots included.

DILL PESTO

2 large garlic cloves, halved and bashed with the flat side of a large knife
2 anchovy fillets in oil, drained and chopped
75g (2½oz) pistachio nuts, dry-roasted until lightly browned (see page 78)
125g (4oz) fresh dill, tough stems removed
75ml (2½fl oz) extra-virgin olive oil
coarsely ground black pepper

BY HAND: pound the garlic and anchovies in a mortar, then add the roasted pistachio nuts and pound to a paste. Pounding and mashing, add the dill a little at a time. Pour in the olive oil in a steady stream and mix until a smooth paste is achieved. Season with black pepper.

MACHINE METHOD: process the garlic, anchovies, nuts, dill and 1 tablespoon of the olive oil until a rough purée is achieved. With the machine running, add the remaining olive oil in a thin, steady stream. Season with black pepper.

OLIVE PESTO

4 large garlic cloves, halved and bashed with the flat side of a large knife
3 tbsp chopped fresh thyme
1 large bunch of fresh flat-leaf parsley, tough stems removed
100g (3½oz) black olives, stoned
75ml (2½fl oz) extra-virgin olive oil

BY HAND: pound the garlic and thyme in a mortar, then, mashing and pounding, add the parsley a handful at a time. Add the olives and pound to a rough purée. Add the olive oil slowly, pounding until a paste is achieved.

MACHINE METHOD: process the garlic, thyme, parsley, olives and 1 tablespoon of the olive oil until a rough paste. With the machine running, add the rest of the olive oil in a thin, steady stream until the paste is smooth.

This is especially good with fish – try drizzling it over smoked salmon canapés.

Shelf-life: 1 week in the refrigerator (make sure there is a protective layer of oil over the pesto), although best eaten immediately

See page 11 for illustration

For this recipe use sun-dried Mediterranean olives.

Shelf-life: *1 week in the refrigerator (make sure there is a protective layer of oil over the pesto), although best eaten immediately*

TAPENADE

This delicious sauce encapsulates the flavours of the Mediterranean. It originated in the south of France – its name comes from the old Provençal word for capers, tapéno. Traditionally the sauce is made with a pestle and mortar, which is not particularly time-consuming but can be strenuous work. Serve this versatile sauce as a dip with raw vegetables, spread on crusty bread or, with plenty of fresh herbs mixed in, as a quick pasta sauce.

Serves 6–8

Shelf-life: *1 month in the refrigerator (make sure there is a protective layer of oil over the tapenade)*

| 50g (1¾oz) anchovy fillets in oil, drained and chopped |
| 2 heaped tbsp capers in vinegar, drained |
| 250g (8oz) good black olives, stoned |
| 4–6 tbsp virgin olive oil |
| lemon juice to taste |

BY HAND: pound the anchovies and capers to a paste in a heavy mortar. Add the olives a few at a time and pound until completely crushed. Start adding the olive oil a little at a time, as if making mayonnaise, and pound until all the oil is used and the mixture is homogeneous. Add the lemon juice and mix well.

MACHINE METHOD: process the capers, anchovies and olives for a few seconds until roughly chopped but not puréed. With the machine running, pour in the oil in a thin, steady stream. Mix in the lemon juice.

ANCHOÏADE

Traditionally spread on bread and browned in the oven, this southern French paste can be served as a sauce for grilled fish or meat, or just mixed with pasta. Use anchovy fillets preserved in oil or whole, salt-preserved anchovies.

Serves 6–8

Shelf-life: *1 month in the refrigerator (make sure there is a protective layer of oil over the anchoïade)*

| 200g (7oz) anchovy fillets in oil, drained and chopped, or salt-preserved anchovy fillets, soaked in water for 20 minutes, then rinsed and chopped |
| 3 tbsp extra-virgin olive oil |
| 100g (3½oz) shallots, finely chopped |
| 2–3 tbsp lemon juice |
| a few gratings of lemon zest |
| 6 tbsp chopped fresh flat-leaf parsley |

Pound the anchovies to a smooth paste in a mortar, or process in a food processor. Gradually mix in the olive oil, then add the rest of the ingredients and mix well.

SIMPLE SALSA VERDE

| 50g (1¾oz) good white bread, torn into small pieces or breadcrumbs |
| 4 tbsp wine vinegar or lemon juice |
| 5–6 tbsp extra-virgin olive oil |
| 2 tbsp capers in vinegar, drained, or 4 anchovy fillets in oil, drained and chopped |
| 8 tbsp chopped fresh mixed herbs, such as flat-leaf parsley, mint and basil |
| 1 tbsp sugar |
| salt and freshly ground black pepper |

Mix all the ingredients together in a bowl and set aside to stand for about 1 hour before serving.

A classic northern Italian sauce, salsa verde, or green sauce, makes a delicious, sharp and refreshing accompaniment to grilled cheese, meat, poultry or fish. For a smoother texture, use breadcrumbs.

Serves 6–8

Shelf-life: *1 month in the refrigerator (make sure there is a protective layer of oil over the salsa verde)*

VARIATION

AGRODOLCE (SWEET & SOUR SALSA VERDE)
Follow the recipe above but omit the sugar and add 100g (3½oz) chopped raisins.

SKORDALIA

| 300g (10oz) floury potatoes |
| 8–10 garlic cloves, crushed |
| lemon juice or vinegar to taste |
| 150–250ml (5–8fl oz) olive oil |
| salt and freshly ground black pepper |

1 Boil the potatoes in their skins until tender. Allow to cool, then peel and cut into even-sized chunks.

2 Tip the potato chunks into a food processor and process to a smooth paste. Add the garlic and lemon juice or vinegar, then, with the machine running, add the oil in a thin, steady stream until the mixture reaches the consistency of soft mashed potato.

3 Season to taste with salt and pepper, then set aside for at least half an hour to allow the flavours to develop.

A superbly garlicky sauce of Greek origin, this is traditionally served as part of a mezze. It makes a delicious dip with raw vegetables but can also be served with grilled fish or poultry. Skordalia can be made with bread instead of potatoes: soak 300g (10oz) white bread, crusts removed, in cold water, then squeeze dry.

Serves 6–8

Shelf-life: *3 days in the refrigerator*

ROMESCO ▷

This Spanish sauce gets its name from the romesco peppers that are traditionally used to make it. Serve as a dip, or as a sauce for chicken, meat or fish. If romesco or other dried peppers are not available, use 3 fresh red peppers, roasted and peeled (see page 96), and a little chilli powder.

Shelf-life: *1 week in the refrigerator; 6 months in a sealed jar (see pages 134–35)*

3 medium fleshy cooking tomatoes

4 garlic cloves, unpeeled

3 dried romesco peppers or other dried sweet peppers, stems removed, deseeded and soaked in hot water for 30 minutes

75g (2½oz) blanched almonds, dry-roasted until golden (see page 78)

3 tbsp white or red wine vinegar

150ml (¼pint) extra-virgin olive oil

salt and freshly ground black pepper

1 Place the tomatoes and garlic in a roasting tin and roast in an oven preheated to 220°C/425°F/Gas Mark 7 for about 15 minutes or until soft. Set aside until cool, then peel the tomatoes and squeeze the softened garlic from its papery skin.

2 Drain and coarsely chop the peppers and process in a blender or food processor with the garlic and almonds, or pound in a mortar. Add the tomatoes and vinegar and process or pound to a purée.

3 Finally, add the olive oil in a thin, steady stream and blend until smooth. Season to taste.

ROUILLE

A classic French condiment traditionally served with bouillabaisse or other fish soups. I use it at the table to add piquancy and a garlic flavour to many dishes. If you prefer a thicker consistency, reduce the amount of stock or omit it altogether.

Shelf-life: *1 week in the refrigerator; 6 months in a sealed jar (see pages 134–35)*

4 large garlic cloves, peeled

2 red peppers, roasted, peeled and deseeded (see page 96), or tinned red pimentos

2–4 red chillies, roasted, peeled and deseeded (see page 96)

60g (2oz) fresh breadcrumbs

3 tbsp olive oil

3 tbsp Fish or Chicken Stock (see pages 30 and 28) (optional)

Process the garlic, red peppers and chillies in a food processor, or pound in a mortar. Mix in the breadcrumbs and olive oil, then add the fish or chicken stock, if using.

RIGHT: ROMESCO BEING PROCESSED UNTIL SMOOTH

TARATOR

This is part of a large family of ancient Middle Eastern and Mediterranean sauces that have nut purées as a base. Serve it as a side sauce with chicken, fish, meat or vegetables, or as a dip. Tarator can be made with pine nuts, hazelnuts or almonds instead of walnuts but be sure to roast the nuts lightly first to enhance their flavour. Use fresh walnuts as older ones can be bitter.

Shelf-life: 1 week in the refrigerator

2 garlic cloves, peeled
125g (4oz) fresh walnuts, lightly dry-roasted (see page 78)
2 slices of white bread, crusts removed, soaked in cold water and squeezed dry
strained juice of 1/2 lemon
100ml (3¹/₂fl oz) olive oil or Chicken Stock (see page 28)
salt

Process the garlic, walnuts, bread and lemon juice in a food processor. With the machine running, slowly pour in the oil or stock and mix until the sauce is smooth. Season with salt. Alternatively, use a pestle and mortar to pound the ingredients.

VARIATION

PISTACHIO TARATOR

Use pistachios instead of walnuts, and flavour with ¹/₂ teaspoon ground cardamom and 3 tablespoons chopped fresh mint. Serve with lamb.

MUHAMMRA

A hot and piquant Middle Eastern sauce of Syrian origin. Serve as part of a mezze, as a dip with toasted pitta bread or to accompany savoury pastries or fritters.

Shelf-life: 2 weeks in the refrigerator; 6 months in a sealed jar (see pages 134–35)

150g (5oz) walnuts, lightly dry-roasted (see page 78)
125ml (4fl oz) extra-virgin olive oil
3–5 red chillies, roasted, peeled and deseeded (see page 96), or 1–2 tbsp chilli powder moistened with 1 tbsp water
5 red peppers, roasted, peeled and deseeded (see page 96)
1–2 slices of dry white bread, crumbled, or 2–4 tbsp dry white breadcrumbs
3–4 tbsp pomegranate molasses, or 4 tbsp lemon or lime juice and 1 tsp dark sugar
1 tsp ground cumin
1 tsp ground allspice or ¹/₂ tsp ground cloves
salt

Process the walnuts and 2 tablespoons of the oil in a food processor until a coarse purée. Add the chillies and peppers and mix until roughly chopped. Transfer to a bowl and mix in the rest of the ingredients.

MALAY PEANUT SAUCE

1 onion, peeled
2.5cm (1 inch) fresh galangal
2 lemongrass stalks, hard outer layers removed
2.5cm (1 inch) fresh ginger
2–4 fresh or dried red chillies, deseeded
4 tbsp groundnut oil
75g (2¹/₂oz) tamarind pulp, soaked in 250ml (8fl oz) hot water, sieved (see below)
2–3 tbsp palm sugar or light brown sugar
250g (8oz) peanuts, roasted, skinned and coarsely ground, or 250g (8oz) coarse peanut butter
2–3 tbsp Thai fish sauce (*nam pla*), or salt to taste

1 Put the onion, galangal, lemongrass, ginger and chillies in a food processor and process to a smooth paste.

2 Heat the oil in a pan, then add the paste and fry, stirring and scraping, for about 10 minutes, until fragrant and nicely browned. Add the tamarind water and bring to the boil. Simmer for about 10 minutes, then add the remaining ingredients and simmer until the sauce has thickened, about 5–10 minutes. Serve warm.

A wonderfully fragrant sauce that is traditionally served with satay, but I also like it with grilled meat or fish or as a dip (hot or cold) for raw or steamed vegetables. If galangal is not available, double the amount of ginger. If peanuts are not available, use a good, crunchy peanut butter, preferably salt- and sugar-free.

Shelf-life: 1 week in the refrigerator

MAKING TAMARIND WATER

1 Pour boiling water over the tamarind pulp in a bowl and mix well. Leave to soak for 15–20 minutes, mixing and mashing with a fork from time to time.

2 Pour the mixture into a sieve set over a bowl, pushing through as much of the pulp as possible. Discard the seeds and tough pulp in the sieve.

HOT ANCHOVY BUTTER

A hot and garlicky dipping sauce for prawns or steamed vegetables.

Advance preparation: the garlic butter can be made in advance

Shelf-life: 1 week in the refrigerator; 3 months in the freezer

1 quantity of Garlic Butter (see page 75)

50g (1¾oz) anchovy fillets in oil, drained and finely chopped

strained juice of 1 lemon

a few scrapings of lemon zest

salt, if necessary, and freshly ground black pepper

Place all the ingredients in a small pan and heat gently until the butter has melted and is hot; be careful not to let it burn. Remove from the heat and keep hot at the table on a burner.

HOT PIRI-PIRI BUTTER

A classic African-Portuguese hot butter sauce traditionally served with prawns. It is a dipping sauce, so is best brought to the table in the pan and kept warm on a small burner.

Shelf-life: 1 week in the refrigerator; 3 months in the freezer

150g (5oz) unsalted butter

strained juice of 1 lemon

a few scrapings of lemon zest

1–3 or more piri-piri chillies, chopped, or chilli powder to taste

1–2 garlic cloves, crushed (optional)

salt

Place all the ingredients in a small pan and heat gently until the butter has melted and is hot; be careful not to let it burn. Remove from the heat and serve hot.

TAMARIND DIPPING SAUCE

Tart and fruity, this dipping sauce is delicious with vegetables, meat, chicken or fish kebabs, or with fried pastries. Tamarind is available as a pulp, a paste or a smooth molasses but I find that the pulp gives the best flavour.

See page 13 for illustration

100g (3½oz) tamarind pulp soaked in 200ml (7fl oz) hot water, sieved (see left)

5 spring onions, finely chopped

1–2 red or green chillies, deseeded and finely chopped

1 small bunch of fresh coriander, chopped

Allow the tamarind water to cool to room temperature. In a small bowl, mix it with the spring onions, chillies and coriander.

CHINESE DIPPING SAUCE

4 tbsp soy sauce

3 tbsp rice vinegar

1 garlic clove, finely chopped

1 tbsp sugar

1cm (½ inch) fresh ginger, finely shredded

2 spring onions, finely shredded

2–3 tbsp Chilli Oil (see page 71, or use commercial chilli oil)

Mix all the ingredients together in a small bowl.

An interesting combination of hot and sweet, this sauce is perfect for dipping dumplings, fried savoury pastries or fried tofu.

THAI DIPPING SAUCE

2 tbsp dark soy sauce

2–3 tbsp Thai fish sauce (*nam pla*)

3 tbsp rice vinegar

1–2 tsp palm sugar or light brown sugar

1 lemongrass stalk, hard outer layers removed, finely chopped

2 red Thai chillies or fresh red bird's eye chillies, sliced into thin rings

2 kaffir lime leaves, shredded

Mix all the ingredients together in a small bowl.

This is quick and easy to make. It is traditionally served as a dipping sauce for fried savoury pastries and pies but is also delicious spooned over rice or noodles.

See page 15 for illustration

CLASSIC VIETNAMESE DIPPING SAUCE

3 tbsp Thai fish sauce (*nam pla*)

4 tbsp lime juice

1 tsp grated lime zest

2–3 hot chillies, deseeded and finely chopped

2 garlic cloves, crushed

1 small carrot, finely shredded

Mix all the ingredients together in a small bowl.

This sharp and hot sauce is traditionally served with fried foods but it is also good just poured over sizzling-hot, grilled or barbecued fish or poultry.

DESSERT SAUCES

DESSERTS JUST WOULDN'T BE THE SAME WITHOUT THESE SIMPLE BUT DELICIOUS SAUCES. POURED OVER

SPONGES, STEAMED PUDDINGS, FRUIT TARTS OR ICE-CREAM, THEY PROVIDE AN ESSENTIAL FINISHING TOUCH.

TRY FLAVOURING A SMOOTH CRÈME ANGLAISE WITH SUBTLE AROMATICS, FRUIT PURÉE OR LIQUEURS; USING A

FROTHY ZABAGLIONE TO TRANSFORM A SIMPLE FRUIT SALAD; OR DRIZZLING A GLORIOUSLY RICH CHOCOLATE

SAUCE OVER PROFITEROLES. ALL THE FAVOURITES ARE HERE, AS WELL AS SOME IRRESISTIBLE NEW CREATIONS.

CRÈME ANGLAISE

Velvety and smooth, crème anglaise, or custard, is the classic dessert sauce and a base for many other sweet sauces and desserts. It can be served hot or chilled, poured over fruit or puddings, or even used as a tart filling. For extra richness replace half or all the milk with single or double cream. Custards can be flavoured in a multitude of ways (see right). See page 40 for the Crème Anglaise master recipe.

Shelf-life: 3 days in the refrigerator

500ml (17fl oz) milk
1 vanilla pod, sliced in half lengthways, or 1 tsp natural vanilla extract
6 egg yolks
3–4 tbsp caster sugar

1 Infuse the milk: scrape the seeds from the vanilla pod, if using, and add both the seeds and the pod or, alternatively, the extract to the milk in a pan. Bring to the boil.

2 In a bowl, whisk the egg yolks and sugar together until the mixture has lightened and become foamy. Still whisking, pour in the boiling milk.

3 Either place the bowl over a pan of just-simmering water, making sure the base of the bowl does not touch the water, or transfer the mixture, together with the vanilla pod, if using, to the top of a double boiler. Stir continuously until the sauce is thick enough to coat the back of the spoon, about 10–15 minutes. Do not allow the custard to boil. Remove the vanilla pod, if using, then whisk well.

VARIATIONS

CHOCOLATE CUSTARD *See page 19 for illustration*
Melt 90g (3oz) good-quality dark chocolate in a bowl set over a pan of simmering water. When the Crème Anglaise has cooled a little, stir in the melted chocolate and 2 tablespoons chocolate liqueur.

BRANDY CUSTARD
Leave the Crème Anglaise to cool a little, then stir in 2–3 tablespoons of good brandy or Cognac. Alternatively, use rum or gin to flavour the custard.

BERRY CUSTARD ▷
Set the Crème Anglaise aside to cool a little. Purée 75–100g (2½–3½oz) fresh berries of your choice, such as raspberries, blueberries or blackberries and stir into the custard with sugar to taste. Stir in an appropriate liqueur, if desired.

HONEY CUSTARD
Instead of infusing the milk with vanilla, add 1 small piece of cinnamon stick, 1–2 bay leaves and 3–4 tablespoons good, fragrant honey, such as lavender or wild-flower honey.

CARAMEL CUSTARD
Reduce the amount of sugar to 2 tablespoons and add 3–4 tablespoons crushed dark caramel (see page 41) to the milk along with the vanilla.

OPPOSITE: STIRRING FRESH RASPBERRY PURÉE INTO CRÈME ANGLAISE

SUGAR SYRUP

This sparkling clear liquor is the sweet equivalent of savoury stocks. Use it to dilute fruit coulis, for cooking fruit, to moisten sponges or as a base for water ices and sorbets. With keeping, sugar syrup can crystallize but adding liquid glucose prevents this happening.

Shelf-life: *3 weeks in the refrigerator*

500g (1lb) caster sugar
450ml ($^3/_4$ pint) water
50g ($1^3/_4$oz) liquid glucose (optional)

1 Put the sugar, water and glucose, if using, in a pan and heat gently, stirring continuously to dissolve the sugar. When all the sugar has dissolved (undissolved sugar will cause crystallization), increase the heat and bring the mixture to the boil.

2 Boil for 2–3 minutes or until the mixture is clear, skimming any scum from the surface if necessary. If the syrup is too thin, go on boiling until the right density is achieved, then remove from the heat.

3 The syrup is ready to use but can also be infused with flavour following one of the three methods below.

VARIATIONS

AROMATICS
Use this method for flavourings such as cloves, cinnamon sticks, allspice, vanilla pods or cardamom. Add about 1 tablespoon of the crushed aromatic of your choice to the finished sugar syrup and simmer for about 15 minutes. Set aside to cool, then filter (see page 135).

ZESTS & FLOWERS
Maceration is the most suitable method for flavouring with lemon or orange zest or lavender flowers: place 60–75g (2–$2^1/_2$oz) of the zest or flowers in a sterilized jar (see page 134) and pour over the hot sugar syrup. Set aside to cool, then filter (see page 135).

FLOWER WATERS, ESSENCES & LIQUEURS
Use this method for flavouring with flower waters such as orange and rose; vanilla extract or bitter almond; rum, kirsch, brandy or any flavoured liqueurs. Set the sugar syrup aside to cool, then stir in 2–3 tablespoons (or more to taste) of the flavouring of your choice.

ZABAGLIONE

4 egg yolks
50g ($1^3/_4$oz) caster sugar
2–3 drops of natural vanilla extract
zest of $^1/_2$ lemon or orange (optional)
100ml ($3^1/_2$fl oz) marsala, or any strong-flavoured sweet white wine

1 Place the egg yolks and sugar in a large bowl and beat either by hand or with an electric beater until the mixture begins to whiten a little. Add the vanilla extract, lemon or orange zest, if using, and marsala and beat until well mixed.

2 Place the bowl over a pan of just-simmering water, making sure the base of the bowl does not touch the water, and whisk until the sauce is thick and frothy, about 10–12 minutes. Serve immediately.

3 To serve zabaglione cold, put the bowl in a larger bowl filled with ice and beat gently until it is cold.

The crowning glory of the Italian dessert table, this frothy, velvet-smooth sauce is extremely versatile. Served warm, it makes a glorious sauce for fruit tarts and salads; poured into elegant glasses, it can be served with crisp biscuits as a warm dessert. It can also be eaten cold or frozen as an ice-cream-like dessert. To make a lighter version, use only 2 egg yolks and 1 whole egg.

Shelf-life: *1 month in the freezer*

VARIATION

BLUEBERRY OR MANGO ZABAGLIONE
In a small pan simmer 100g ($3^1/_2$oz) fresh blueberries or cubed fresh mango with 3–4 tablespoons water or wine until soft. Purée the fruit in a food processor or blender until smooth, then pass through a sieve, using the back of a spoon to push the mixture through. Stir the fruit purée into the finished zabaglione and serve.

YOGURT & HONEY SAUCE

250ml (8fl oz) Greek-style yogurt, well chilled
1–2 tbsp chopped fresh eau de Cologne mint (use any fresh mint if this is not available)
3 tbsp fragrant clear honey

Place the yogurt in a bowl and stir in the mint. Drizzle the honey on top and fold in very carefully to achieve a marbled effect. Using very cold yogurt will improve the marbled effect.

A startlingly simple yet delicious sauce, this is best served very cold, spooned over hot pancakes, steamed puddings or fresh fruit. For an extra-rich sauce use thick double cream or crème fraîche instead of yogurt.

BANANA CARAMEL SAUCE

A rich, luscious and very delicious sauce. Serve hot or cold, with ice-cream or flans, or poured over waffles or pancakes. A halved and scraped vanilla pod can be used instead of the cinnamon.

3 ripe bananas, peeled and sliced

a few gratings of lemon zest

strained juice of 1 lemon

60g (2oz) butter

4 tbsp soft dark brown sugar

1 tsp ground cinnamon

250ml (8fl oz) single cream

2–3 tbsp rum

1 Put the bananas and lemon zest in a bowl, add the lemon juice and mix to coat the bananas in the juice.

2 Melt the butter in a pan, add the sugar and heat gently, stirring constantly, until all the sugar has dissolved.

3 Add the bananas in lemon juice and the cinammon and cook for 10–12 minutes, until the bananas are soft and have started to disintegrate.

4 Tip everything into a blender or food processor and process to a smooth purée. Add the cream and process to blend.

5 Either reheat to boiling point or set aside to cool, then refrigerate and serve cold. Stir in the rum just before serving.

PINEAPPLE & GINGER SAUCE

1 medium pineapple, peeled, cored and chopped

200g (7oz) caster sugar

4 tbsp white wine or fruit juice

4–5 bitter almonds or ¹/₂ tsp of almond extract (optional)

1 vanilla pod, sliced in half lengthways

60g (2oz) chopped preserved stem ginger, soaked in 2 tbsp rum or kirsch for 30 minutes

An aromatic, sweet and sour sauce that goes very well with fruit tarts, ice-cream and soufflés. For the best flavour make sure you use a very ripe pineapple. You can substitute mango for the pineapple, in which case use two large mangoes and reduce the sugar to taste.

1 Put all but about 75g (2¹/₂oz) of the pineapple in a pan, add the sugar, white wine or fruit juice and bitter almonds or almond extract, if using. Scrape the seeds from the vanilla pod and add both the seeds and the pod to the pan. Bring to the boil, then reduce the heat and simmer until the pineapple is tender, about 20 minutes.

2 Remove from the heat and fish out the vanilla pod and the bitter almonds, if using. Transfer the mixture to a blender and process for 1–2 minutes, until smooth.

3 Return the mixture to the pan, bring to the boil, then reduce the heat and simmer until the sauce has thickened slightly.

4 Chop the reserved pineapple finely and stir into the sauce with the ginger and rum or kirsch. Serve hot or cold.

RAISIN SAUCE

Serve this easy sauce with hot or cold fruit tarts.

400ml (14fl oz) fragrant, fruity white wine such as Gewürztraminer

150g (5oz) seedless golden raisins, coarsely chopped

strained juice of 1 lemon

1–2 tbsp honey or caster sugar, or more to taste

75ml (2¹/₂fl oz) double cream

30g (1oz) unsalted butter, or Brandy Butter (see page 133), chilled and cubed

2 tbsp rum

In a small pan simmer the wine, raisins, lemon juice and honey or sugar until the raisins are plump, about 20 minutes. Tip into a blender or food processor and process until smooth. Return the mixture to a clean pan, bring to the boil and whisk in the cream, then the butter a little at a time. Finish by stirring in the rum.

ORANGE & RED WINE SAUCE

This deliciously spicy sauce is wonderful poured over flans and tarts and, of course, ice-cream. If blood oranges are not available, use 2 large oranges. Serve hot or cold.

Shelf-life: *1 month in the refrigerator*

strained juice of 4 blood oranges
250ml (8fl oz) full-bodied, fruity red wine
4 tbsp soft brown sugar
½ cinnamon stick, 3 cloves and 4–5 allspice berries, tied in a square of muslin
thinly pared zest of 1 orange, cut into thin julienne
1 tsp cornflour, dissolved in 2 tbsp orange juice or red wine
30g (1oz) unsalted butter, or Orange Butter (see page 133), chilled and cubed

1 Put the orange juice, wine and sugar in a small pan with the spice bag, bring to the boil and simmer until the mixture has reduced by a third, about 15–20 minutes. Remove the spice bag. In a separate pan, blanch the orange zest in boiling water for 1 minute, then drain, refresh in cold water and drain again.

2 Add the cornflour to the wine mixture and simmer for a minute, until thickened slightly. Beat in the blanched orange zest and the butter, a little at a time.

PASSION FRUIT SAUCE

Tart and fragrant, this sauce is very easy to make. Serve it hot or cold over cakes and flans or to top ice-cream, soufflés or cheesecakes. The passion fruit seeds add texture and visual interest to this wonderful sauce.

Shelf-life: *1 week in the refrigerator*

1 tsp arrowroot
strained juice of 3 oranges
3–4 tbsp caster sugar or more to taste
½ tsp grated lemon zest
6 passion fruit, cut in half
30g (1oz) unsalted butter, chilled and cubed

1 Dissolve the arrowroot in 2 tablespoons of the orange juice and set aside. Put the remaining orange juice, the sugar and lemon zest in a small pan and boil until reduced by half.

2 Scoop the passion fruit pulp and seeds into the pan and bring to the boil again. Boil for about 1 minute, then add the arrowroot and boil for a further minute until thickened slightly. Beat in the butter a little at a time.

MAPLE PECAN SAUCE

200ml (7fl oz) maple syrup
100ml (3½fl oz) double cream
1 tbsp good instant coffee, dissolved in 2 tbsp boiling water
75g (2½oz) pecan nuts, lightly roasted, chopped
1–2 tbsp coffee liqueur (optional)

This North American classic depends on the quality of the maple syrup; buy the real thing and avoid maple-flavour substitutes. Serve over ice-cream, steamed puddings or simply poured on hot waffles or pancakes.

1 In a small pan, bring the maple syrup and cream to the boil, then reduce the heat to medium and simmer, stirring frequently, until slightly reduced, about 5 minutes.

2 Remove from the heat and allow to cool a little, then stir in the coffee, the nuts and the liqueur, if using.

COOKED FRUIT COULIS

300g (10oz) soft fruit, such as raspberries, strawberries or blackberries, or 500g (1lb) fruit, such as cherries or plums, stoned
400ml (14fl oz) water
100–150g (3½–5oz) caster sugar, to taste
strained juice of ½ lemon
60ml (2fl oz) liqueur (optional)

A simple classic that is extremely versatile and can be served chilled or warm to add moisture and contrasting flavour to any dessert. You could substitute other fruit, such as mangos, papaya or pineapple, as long as the weight after stoning and peeling is 300g (10oz). Choose a liqueur that complements the fruit.

Shelf-life: *1 week in the refrigerator*

1 Place the fruit, water, sugar and lemon juice in a pan. Bring to the boil, then reduce the heat and simmer for 20–25 minutes or until the fruit is soft and mushy and beginning to disintegrate.

2 Remove from the heat, transfer the mixture to a blender or food processor and process until smooth. Pass the sauce through a fine sieve, stir in the liqueur, if using, and chill.

VARIATION

FRESH FRUIT COULIS
A fresh version of the recipe above, this works best with soft fruit. Put the fruit and liqueur in a food processor with 250ml (8fl oz) Sugar Syrup (see page 128). Process until smooth, then pass through a fine sieve and serve chilled.

OPPOSITE, CLOCKWISE FROM TOP LEFT: ORANGE & RED WINE SAUCE, MAPLE PECAN SAUCE, COOKED FRUIT COULIS AND PASSION FRUIT SAUCE, ALL WITH ICE-CREAM

SIMPLE CHOCOLATE SAUCE

Use the best-quality chocolate you can find, with as high a cocoa solids content as possible – many supermarkets now sell a 70% cocoa solids bar. For a richer sauce, replace the milk with single or double cream. Vary the flavour by adding brandy, rum or flavoured liqueurs such as Grand Marnier, mint or almond, or use flavouring essences such as rose water, orange flower or vanilla.

Shelf-life: *1 week in the refrigerator (reheat gently in a bowl placed over a pan of simmering water)*

200g (7oz) good-quality dark chocolate
75ml (2½fl oz) milk
75ml (2½fl oz) double or single cream
2–3 tbsp caster sugar or to taste

1 Break the chocolate into pieces and put in a bowl placed over a pan of simmering water, making sure the base of the bowl does not touch the water. Leave to melt, stirring occasionally.

2 Put the milk, cream and sugar in a pan and bring to the boil. Gently pour the hot milk and cream mixture on to the melted chocolate and whisk until smooth. Either serve hot or set aside to cool, whisking from time to time to prevent a skin forming.

WHITE CHOCOLATE SAUCE

This is a simple chocolate sauce with a hint of orange. Use with the Simple Chocolate Sauce above to create a striking black and white effect.

Shelf-life: *1 week in the refrigerator (reheat gently in a bowl placed over a pan of simmering water)*

200g (7oz) good-quality white chocolate, broken into pieces
200ml (7fl oz) double cream
100ml (3½fl oz) milk
1–2 strips orange zest (optional)

1 Melt the chocolate in a bowl placed over a pan of simmering water, making sure the base of the bowl does not touch the water. Stir until smooth.

2 Put the cream, milk and orange zest, if using, in a small pan and bring to the boil. Reduce the heat and simmer for 2–3 minutes, then remove the orange zest.

3 Gently pour the hot cream and milk mixture on to the melted chocolate and whisk until smooth. Serve the sauce warm or set aside to cool and serve at room temperature.

FUDGE SAUCE

400ml (14fl oz) evaporated milk
75–100g (2½–3½oz) caster sugar
1 vanilla pod, sliced in half lengthways, or 1 tsp natural vanilla extract
150g (5oz) good-quality dark chocolate, broken into pieces
30g (1oz) unsalted butter
a pinch of salt

This is traditionally served with ice-cream but it can also be poured over steamed puddings or served as a tart filling.

Shelf-life: *1 month in the refrigerator*

1 Heat the evaporated milk, sugar and vanilla pod or extract in a pan over a medium heat, stirring to dissolve the sugar. Bring to a rolling boil and boil for 1 minute, stirring constantly.

2 Remove from the heat and fish out the vanilla pod, if using. Scrape the seeds from the pod and add them to the milk; discard the pod. Add the chocolate and whisk until it has melted. Add the butter and salt and whisk until smooth. Serve hot or cold.

VARIATIONS

RICH FUDGE SAUCE
Substitute 250ml (8fl oz) double cream for the evaporated milk and 75–100g (2½–3½oz) light brown sugar such as demerara for the caster sugar. Omit the vanilla and the salt and stir in ½ teaspoon ground cinnamon.

NUT FUDGE SAUCE
Stir 75g (2½oz) chopped, lightly toasted pecans or almonds into Fudge Sauce or Rich Fudge Sauce.

GINGER FUDGE SAUCE
Flavour Fudge Sauce or Rich Fudge Sauce with ½ tsp ground ginger and 50g (1¾oz) chopped stem ginger.

BRANDY FUDGE SAUCE
Stir 2 tablespoons good brandy or rum into the finished Fudge Sauce or Rich Fudge Sauce.

SWEET BUTTERS

MELT SWEET BUTTERS ON HOT PANCAKES, waffles or puddings or use them as a simple filling and frosting for sponge cakes. I add them where I would normally use plain butter, to give flavour, richness and gloss to dessert sauces. I don't like my butters too sweet and use 75g (2½oz) sugar to 100g (3½oz) butter, but you can increase the sugar to 100g (3½oz) or more if you have a sweet tooth. Sweet butters can be made by hand but an electric beater will produce lighter and fluffier results.

BRANDY BUTTER

This famous sweet butter is the traditional accompaniment to Christmas pudding.

Shelf-life: 2 weeks in the refrigerator; 3 months in the freezer

100g (3½oz) unsalted butter, softened
75g (2½oz) caster sugar
2–3 tbsp brandy
a few drops of lemon juice (optional)
½ tsp grated lemon zest (optional)

Cream the butter and sugar together until white and fluffy. Add the brandy, lemon juice and zest, if using, and beat until well mixed. Place the butter on a piece of greaseproof paper and roll into a cylinder shape (see page 74). Chill until firm.

VARIATIONS

ORANGE BUTTER
Substitute an orange liqueur such as Cointreau, Grand Marnier or triple sec for the brandy. Add 1 teaspoon grated orange zest instead of the lemon juice and zest.

CHERRY BUTTER ▷
Substitute cherry brandy, kirsch or any other cherry liqueur for the brandy and mix in 50g (1¾oz) chopped fresh or glacé cherries. Omit the lemon juice and zest.

RUM & GINGER BUTTER *See page 23 for illustration*
Substitute dark molasses sugar for the caster sugar (or, for a softer, lighter butter, use demerara or muscovado sugar). Use a good-quality rum instead of the brandy and mix in 30g (1oz) chopped stem ginger.

RIGHT: CHERRY BUTTER MELTING ON HOT WAFFLES

KEEPING & FREEZING

THESE ARE SIMPLE METHODS of extending the shelf-life of some sauces. You can preserve many of the sauces in this book in sterilized jars in the refrigerator but any with low acidity or a low sugar or salt content need to be heat processed, especially if you want to keep them for longer than three or four months.

STERILIZING JARS

A CONVENIENT AND EFFECTIVE WAY to sterilize jars is to boil them. Once sterilized, the jars are suitable for bottling and storing food. Special clamp-top jars are easily available (always use new rubber rings), but you can also use screw-top jars, many of which have a rubber seal.

Wash the jars thoroughly in hot, soapy water before you begin, then place a cake rack or upturned saucer in the bottom of a large pan to prevent the jars from touching the base and cracking. When placing jars in the pan, make sure that they do not touch each other or the sides of the pan during boiling.

After boiling, remove the pan from the heat, lift the jars out with tongs and drain upside down on clean kitchen towel. Place the jars on a kitchen towel-lined baking tray and dry in a cool oven.

1 Put a cake rack or upturned saucer in the bottom of a pan. Put the jars, lids and any rubber seals on top, fill with hot water until they are completely immersed and boil rapidly for 10 minutes. Drain, upside down, on kitchen towel.

2 Dry in a cool oven on a kitchen towel-lined baking tray. Once sterilized, reassemble each jar. Attach the new, sterilized rubber ring, if using, by placing it on the lid of the jar, then stretching and fitting it into place.

HEAT PROCESSING

THE PROCESS OF BOILING and then cooling the filled jars causes the contents to contract and form a vacuum; this seals the food in and prevents it from coming into contact with oxygen, thus preserving it.

To boil, wrap each filled jar in a few layers of cloth, such as an old tea towel, or newspaper to prevent the jars from knocking against each other. Place a cake rack or an upturned saucer in the bottom of a large pan to prevent the jars from touching the base, and put the jars on top. Fill, to cover, with water, and check the water level from time to time, topping it up as necessary.

When heat processed for the recommended time (see chart opposite), remove the pan from the heat and lift the jars out with tongs. Set aside to cool completely, then check the seal (see Tips for Keeping, opposite).

1 Fill the hot, sterilized jars to within 1cm (½ inch) of the top with the hot or cold sauce. Clamp the lid shut. Wrap the jars in cloth (see left) and place in a pan on a cake rack or upturned saucer.

2 Pour in enough hot water to cover the lids of the jars by at least 2.5cm (1 inch). Cover the pan, bring to the boil and boil for the recommended time (see chart opposite).

HEAT PROCESSING TIMES

All the times are counted from the moment the water comes back to the boil.

Heat processing times for cold-packed preserves

500g (1lb) jars – 25 minutes

600ml (1 pint) bottles – 25 minutes

1kg (2lb) jars – 30 minutes

1 litre (1¾ – 2 pint) bottles – 30 minutes

Heat processing times for hot-packed preserves

500g (1lb) jars – 20 minutes

600ml (1 pint) bottles – 20 minutes

1kg (2lb) jars – 25 minutes

1 litre (1¾ – 2 pint) bottles – 25 minutes

TIPS FOR KEEPING

To test a seal on a clamp-top jar
Gently unclamp the lid and slowly lift the jar holding just the lid – if sealed it will support the weight.

To test a seal on a one-piece lidded jar
Check for a dip in the middle of the lid – this shows that a vacuum has formed.

If a seal has not formed
Tip the contents of the jar into a pan and boil for 3–4 minutes. Return to a clean jar and repeat the sterilizing process.

FILTERING

VINEGARS, OILS AND OTHER LIQUIDS can become cloudy and need filtering before storage. Filtering also removes flavouring ingredients.

To filter, carefully pour the liquid through a muslin-lined funnel into a clean bottle.

FREEZING

FREEZING IS THE BUSY COOK'S ANSWER to preserving in jars and is the simplest and most convenient way of extending the storage life of food.

Do not freeze food for longer than recommended in the recipe as this can cause discoloration and may alter the texture and consistency. Label all containers and packages of food, then check the contents of your freezer regularly and discard anything that has outlived its freezing time.

Try to freeze food in convenient quantities – in single portions or in ice cube trays, for example. Freeze only the freshest food that is in perfect condition. When freezing liquids, leave 1cm (½ inch) space at the top of the container to allow for expansion. Cool hot food quickly before freezing it and do not be tempted to put warm food in the freezer as this creates condensation.

Making Ice Cubes
Herb purée, tomato purée and stock can easily be frozen into blocks in ice cube trays. The cubes can then be stored in bags in the freezer and added in convenient quantities while cooking.

Filling Containers
Choose containers that seal tightly and won't leak. Write the contents of the container and the date on a label and stick it on the container.

TROUBLESHOOTING

IF YOU ENCOUNTER PROBLEMS with any of your sauces, the chart below should help you to understand why they may have occurred and, in most cases, to correct what has gone wrong. It also includes tips to help you improve the texture, correct the consistency and enhance the flavour of your sauces.

	PROBLEM	POSSIBLE CAUSE	REMEDY
STOCKS	• Cloudy	• Bones not washed thoroughly; not skimmed well enough; allowed to boil; not allowed to settle	• See Troubleshooting box, page 29
	• Too thin	• Not enough bones; inferior bones; not enough vegetables; not allowed to reduce enough	• Add more bones and vegetables or allow to reduce further
	• Fatty	• Not skimmed well enough	• Chill in the refrigerator and skim well (see page 28)
WHITE SAUCES	• Lumpy	• Not whisked enough; brought to the boil too quickly	• Sieve or process in the blender, then return to the pan and heat to boiling point (see Troubleshooting box, page 32)
	• Too thick	• Reduced too much; not enough milk	• Dilute with a little milk or cream
	• Too thin	• Not reduced enough; too much milk	• Add a little beurre manié (see page 45), bring back to the boil and cook until reduced and thickened
CHEESE SAUCE	• Too thick	• Reduced too much; too much flour in the base sauce; too much cheese	• Dilute with a little milk or cream and heat through
	• Too thin	• Too much liquid; not enough cheese	• Add a little more cheese and heat through
	• Lumpy	• Not whisked enough; cheese has not melted properly	• Return to the heat and whisk until smooth
	• Stringy	• Cooked too long or on too high a heat; the protein of the cheese has cooked and become stringy	• No remedy
VELOUTÉ	• Too thin	• Not enough flour; too much liquid; not reduced enough	• Either reduce further or add 15–30g (½–1oz) beurre manié (see page 45) and whisk well; bring to a simmer and whisk for 3–4 minutes to cook the flour
	• Lumpy	• Not whisked enough	• Pass through a sieve
	• Insipid	• Badly made or flavourless stock; not reduced enough; not enough flavouring	• Adjust seasoning or add some vegetables, reduce further and strain
HOLLANDAISE	• Too thin	• Too little butter; base reduction not reduced enough	• Add more butter
	• Separated	• Cooked too quickly; butter added too quickly	• See Troubleshooting box, page 34
	• Curdled	• Cooked over too high a heat or for too long	• No remedy
BEURRE BLANC & VARIATIONS	• Too thin	• Base reduction not reduced enough; butter not cold enough; not enough butter; not whisked enough	• Remove from the heat and whisk vigorously
	• Separated	• Butter added too quickly; butter not cold enough; cooked over too high a heat	• Add 2–3 tablespoons double cream and bring to a quick boil, reduce for 1–2 minutes, lower the heat and add the separated sauce a spoonful at a time, whisking continuously until the sauce is amalgamated; serve immediately
	• Insipid	• Base reduction not flavoursome enough; poor-quality butter	• Season with a little lemon juice, pepper and/or chilli powder
REDUCTION SAUCES	• Too thin	• Not reduced enough	• Return to the heat and reduce further
	• Too thick	• Reduced too much	• Add a little wine or stock and cook for a further 1–2 minutes
	• Cloudy	• Not skimmed well enough; boiled too quickly in early stages	• Strain through muslin (see Stocks, pages 28–31)
GRAVY	• Too thick	• Too much flour or thickener; reduced too much	• Add a little stock or wine and cook for 1–2 minutes.
	• Too thin	• Not reduced enough; too little flour or thickener	• Either reduce further or add 2 teaspoons or more of beurre manié (see page 45) and cook for 2–3 minutes
	• Lumpy	• Liquid added too quickly; not whisked enough	• Pass through a sieve

	PROBLEM	POSSIBLE CAUSE	REMEDY
VINAIGRETTE	• Separated	• Not whisked enough; left to stand for too long	• Whisk vigorously or start again with 1 teaspoon of mustard and whisk in the separated vinaigrette
	• Too thin	• Too little oil, not enough mustard	• Add some mustard or cream
	• Too sour	• Too much vinegar or lemon juice	• Add some sugar or more oil
OILS	• Off-smelling	• Oil exposed to oxygen	• No remedy, discard
	• Cloudy	• Dirty ingredients; stored at too low a temperature; reaction of oil to ingredients	• Does not affect the flavour, try to remedy by straining through a filter or muslin (see page 135)
MAYONNAISE	• Separated	• Oil added too quickly; not whisked enough	• See Troubleshooting box, page 38
	• Too thick	• Too much oil	• Whisk in a little lemon juice, vinegar, water or cream
	• Too thin	• Not enough oil; too much vinegar or lemon juice	• Whisk in some more oil
COOKING SAUCES	• Too thick	• Cooked too long	• Dilute with an appropriate liquid
	• Too thin	• Too much liquid	• Thicken with beurre manié, cornflour or arrowroot (see pages 44–45) or boil rapidly to reduce
COOKED TOMATO SAUCES	• Too thick	• Cooked too long	• Dilute with a little wine, stock or water
	• Too thin	• Not cooked long enough, tomatoes too watery	• Cook further or thicken with cornflour or arrowroot (see pages 44–45)
	• Bitter or too sour	• Cooked too long; burned; too many herbs and spices; tomatoes too sour	• Sweeten with a little sugar
SALSAS	• Watery	• Vegetables too watery; allowed to stand for too long	• Strain, add breadcrumbs (see page 45) and adjust flavouring
	• Fermented	• Allowed to stand for too long; not enough salt or acidity	• Discard immediately
RELISHES	• Fermented	• Not enough acid or sugar; not cooked enough	• No remedy, discard
	• Mouldy	• Not enough acid or sugar; not cooked enough; stored in an unsterilized container; seal broken	• No remedy, discard
	• Discoloured	• Exposed to light	• Does not affect the flavour
CRÈME ANGLAISE	• Curdled	• Cooked too long or over too high a heat causing the egg protein to cook	• See Troubleshooting. No remedy if eggs completely coagulated
	• Too thin	• Not cooked for long enough	• Cautiously raise the heat and continue to cook
SUGAR SYRUP	• Cloudy	• Dusty sugar; sugar not dissolved properly	• Strain through muslin or clarify with egg as for stock (see Troubleshooting box, page 29)
	• Fermented	• Kept for too long; sugar not concentrated enough	• No remedy, discard
ZABAGLIONE	• Curdled	• Cooked over too high a heat; overworked	• No remedy
	• Too thin	• Too much liquid; not cooked enough	• Cook further while whisking or fold in 1 stiffly beaten egg white
FRUIT COULIS	• Too thick	• Not enough sugar syrup or liquid; not processed fine enough	• Dilute with a little sugar syrup or pass through a sieve
	• Too thin	• Not enough fruit; too much sugar syrup	• Add more puréed fruit or thicken with cornflour or arrowroot (see pages 44–45)
CHOCOLATE SAUCE	• Too thick	• Too much chocolate; too little butter or milk	• Dilute with a little cream or an appropriate liqueur
	• Too thin	• Too little chocolate; not cooked for long enough	• Add some more chocolate; continue to cook
	• Dull	• Poor-quality chocolate; not whisked enough	• Add 1 tablespoon of unflavoured oil or butter and whisk well
	• Hard and stringy	• Cooked over too high a heat	• No remedy
	• Chocolate seizes	• Chocolate coming into contact with water or steam while melting	• Add a little butter or vegetable oil and stir until smooth again

MATCHING SAUCES WITH FOOD

Use this chart to help you partner sauces with basic ingredients and as an inspirational guide for creating imaginative and delicious meals. Don't stop with these suggestions; experiment with different combinations and enjoy sauces for their tremendous versatility whether planning a simple meal or an impressive feast.

SAVOURY SAUCES

Sauce	Poultry	Beef	Pork	Lamb	Fish & shellfish	Vegetables	Salads	Pasta, rice & noodles
Soubise (p.48)		•		•		•		
Caramelized Soubise (p.48)		•		•		•		
Mushroom Sauce (p.49)	•				•	•		•
Robust Mushroom Sauce (p.49)	•	•				•		•
Mornay Sauce (p.49)					•	•		•
Blue Cheese Sauce (p.49)	•	•				•		•
Béchamel (pp.32–3)						•		•
Exotic Béchamel (p.50)	•				•	•		
Aurora (p.50)	•				•	•		
Parsley Sauce (p.50)					•	•		
Mixed Herb Sauce (p.50)	•				•	•		
Velouté (p.52)	•		•	•				
Caper Sauce (p.52)			•	•				
Lemongrass & Coconut Sauce (p.52)	•							
Supreme Sauce (p.53)	•							
Olive Oil Sauce (p.53)	•				•	•		
Mustard Sauce (p.53)	•	•	•	•	•	•		
Béarnaise (p.54)		•		•				
Beurre Blanc (p.54)					•			
Orange Butter Sauce (p.54)	•			•				
Lemongrass Butter Sauce (p.54)	•				•			•
Chilli Butter Sauce (p.54)	•	•			•	•		
Hollandaise (pp.34–5)	•				•	•		
Maltaise (p.55)	•					•		
Exotic Hollandaise (p.55)	•				•	•		
Sabayon (pp.36–7)	•				•	•		
Pink Champagne Sabayon (p.57)					•			
Seafood Sabayon (p.57)					•			
Avgolemono (p.57)	•				•	•		
Orange & Saffron Sabayon (p.57)					•			
Watercress Coulis (p.58)					•	•		
Carrot Coulis (p.58)	•					•		
Avocado Coulis (p.59)	•				•	•		
Fresh Tomato Coulis (p.59)	•					•		•
Cooked Tomato Coulis (p.59)	•	•	•	•	•	•		•
Demi-glace (p.60)		•						
Madeira Demi-glace (p.61)		•						
Red Demi-glace (p.61)		•						
Juniper Demi-glace (p.61)		•		•				
Thickened Demi-glace (p.61)		•						
Wild Mushroom Demi-glace (p.62)		•		•				
Red Wine Sauce (p.62)				•				
Orange & Saffron Sauce (p.62)	•			•				

Sauce	Poultry	Beef	Pork	Lamb	Fish & shellfish	Vegetables	Salads	Pasta, rice & noodles
Ginger & Spring Onion Sauce (p.64)					•			
Lemon Sauce (p.64)					•			
Balsamic Vinegar Sauce (p.64)	•				•			
Traditional Pan Gravy (p.65)	•		•	•				
Tomato Gravy (p.65)	•		•	•				
Mustard Gravy (p.65)	•	•	•					
Gravy for Lamb or Game (p.65)				•		•		
Onion Gravy (p.65)			•	•				
Caramelized Onion Gravy (p.65)	•			•		•		
Blue Cheese Dressing (p.66)		•					•	
Thousand Island Dressing (p.66)		•				•	•	
Feta Cheese Dressing (p.66)						•	•	
Mango Dressing (p.66)	•			•	•	•	•	
Soured Cream Dressing (p.68)						•	•	•
Tahini Sauce (p.68)			•			•	•	
Hazelnut Tahini (p.68)	•					•	•	
Peanut Tahini (p.68)	•					•	•	
Green Tahini (p.68)	•			•		•		
Salad Cream (p.68)						•	•	
Vinaigrette (p.68)						•	•	•
Roquefort Dressing (p.68)		•				•	•	
Garlic & Herb Vinaigrette (p.68)						•	•	
Pepper & Chilli Vinaigrette (p.69)	•					•	•	
Cooked Vinaigrette (p.69)	•					•	•	
Steve's Spicy Vinaigrette (p.69)						•	•	
Raspberry Vinaigrette (p.69)	•					•	•	
Warm Maple Vinaigrette (p.69)	•					•	•	
Herb Oil (p.70)	•	•	•	•	•	•		
Lavender Oil (p.70)				•				
Thai Caramelized Oil (p.70)						•	•	
Lemon Oil (p.70)	•		•		•	•		
Garlic Oil (p.70)	•		•	•	•	•		•
Fresh Chilli Oil (p.71)	•	•	•		•	•		•
Smoky Chilli Oil (p.71)	•	•	•		•	•		
Kaffir Lime Oil (p.71)	•				•		•	•
Mayonnaise (p.72)	•				•		•	
Garlic Mayonnaise (p.72)	•				•	•	•	
Herb Mayonnaise (p.72)	•				•		•	
Smoky Red Pepper Mayonnaise (p.72)	•				•	•	•	
Orange Mustard Mayonnaise (p.72)	•	•			•		•	
Beetroot Mayonnaise (p.72)	•				•		•	•
Harissa Mayonnaise (p.72)	•				•		•	
Prawn Cocktail Sauce (p.72)	•				•		•	•

	Poultry	Beef	Pork	Lamb	Fish & shellfish	Vegetables	Salads	Pasta, rice & noodles
Green Goddess Dressing (p.72)		•			•	•	•	
Gribiche (p.73)		•			•	•	•	
Tartare Sauce (p.73)					•	•		
Yogurttaise (p.73)					•	•	•	
Aïoli (p.73)	•	•	•	•	•	•	•	
Rémoulade (p.73)	•	•	•	•	•	•	•	
Chilli Butter (p.74)	•	•	•	•	•	•		•
Lemongrass & Lime Butter (p.74)	•		•		•	•		•
Tomato Butter (p.74)	•	•	•	•	•	•		•
Anchovy Butter (p.75)		•			•	•		•
Lemon Butter (p.75)	•				•	•		
Garlic Butter (p.75)	•	•	•	•	•	•		•
Spicy Tomato & Chilli Sauce (p.76)					•			
Spicy Tomato & Fennel Sauce (p.76)	•				•			
Spicy Pepper Sauce (p.76)	•	•			•			•
Dry Curry (p.78)	•	•		•	•			
Dry Vegetable Curry (p.79)						•		
Anglo-Indian Curry (p.79)	•	•	•	•	•			
Lamb Korma (p.80)				•				
Chicken Korma (p.80)	•							
Paneer or Tofu Korma (p.80)								
Rogan Josh (p.82)		•		•				
Vanilla Curry (p.82)	•							
Sabzi (p.83)	•	•		•				
Plum Sauce for Fish (p.83)					•			
Sweet & Sour Sauce (p.84)	•		•	•	•			
Fruity Sweet & Sour Sauce (p.84)	•		•	•	•			
Black Bean Sauce (p.84)	•	•	•	•		•		
Red Curry Paste (p.85)		•	•	•				
Yellow Curry Paste (p.85)	•	•	•	•	•			
Green Curry Paste (p.86)	•	•	•	•	•	•		
Light Curry for Fish (p.86)					•			
Mole (p.88)	•			•				
Chilli con Carne (p.89)		•	•					
Manchamantel (p.89)		•	•					
Passata (p.90)	•	•	•		•			•
Arrabbiata (p.90)	•							•
Aubergine Sauce (p.90)			•			•		•
Tomato & Tuna Sauce (p.91)					•			•
Tomato & Grilled Courgette Sauce (p.91)								•
Vongole (p.92)								•
Three-tomato Sauce (p.92)	•				•	•		•
Wild Mushroom Sauce (p.92)	•							•
Creamy Mushroom Sauce (p.92)	•	•						
Three-chilli Salsa (p.94)	•	•			•	•		•
Tomato & Cucumber Salsa (p.94)	•				•	•	•	
Tomato & Pepper Salsa (p.96)	•		•	•	•	•		•
Papaya & Kaffir Lime Salsa (p.96)	•		•	•	•	•		•
Exotic Papaya & Kaffir Lime Salsa (p.96)	•	•	•	•	•	•		•
Beetroot & Apple Salsa (p.96)							•	•
Tomatillo Salsa (p.97)	•	•	•	•	•	•		
Pomegranate & Herb Salsa (p.97)		•			•	•	•	
Guacamole (p.97)	•					•		

	Poultry	Beef	Pork	Lamb	Fish & shellfish	Vegetables	Salads	Pasta, rice & noodles
Mixed Pepper Salsa (p.98)	•	•	•	•		•	•	•
Citrus Salsa (p.98)	•				•	•		
Mango & Tomato Salsa (p.98)	•					•	•	•
Roast Corn Salsa (p.98)	•	•	•			•		
Fresh Onion Chutney (p.100)	•					•	•	
Herb Chutney (p.100)	•				•	•		
Coconut Chutney (p.100)					•		•	•
Cashew Nut Chutney (p.100)	•					•	•	
Green Chilli Chutney (p.101)			•			•	•	
Carrot Chutney (p.101)	•					•	•	
Banana Chutney (p.101)	•	•	•			•	•	
Matbucha (p.102)	•	•				•	•	
Green Chilli Relish (p.102)		•	•	•		•	•	
Harissa (p.103)	•	•		•	•	•		•
Fruity Chilli Relish (p.103)	•					•	•	
Two-tomato Relish (p.103)	•					•	•	
Exotic Fruit Relish (p.103)	•		•				•	
Onion Raita (p.104)						•	•	•
Tomato Raita (p.104)	•		•			•		•
Quince Sambal (p.104)	•	•		•		•		•
Carrot Sambal (p.104)	•	•				•		
Cucumber Sambal (p.104)	•					•	•	
Smoky Aubergine Dip (p.105)	•					•	•	
Pepper & Aubergine Dip (p.105)						•	•	
Feta & Aubergine Dip (p.105)						•	•	
Yogurt, Garlic & Lemon Dip (p.105)						•	•	
Simple Yogurt Dip (p.105)						•	•	
Bean Dip (p.106)							•	
Pepper Dip (p.106)							•	
Taramasalata (p.106)						•	•	
Soured Cream & Saffron Dip (p.106)						•	•	
Lavender Lamb Marinade (p.108)				•				
Mediterranean Fish Marinade (p.108)					•			
Cider & Herb Marinade (p.110)		•	•					
Traditional Barbecue Sauce (p.110)	•	•	•	•				
Barbecue Sauce with Cocoa (p.110)		•	•					
Tandoori Marinade (p.110)	•	•	•					
Orange & Ginger Sauce (p.111)	•	•	•					
Beer Marinade (p.111)		•	•					
Ceviche (p.112)					•			
Tzaramelo (p.112)	•	•	•					
Oriental Soy Marinade (p.113)	•	•	•		•			
Lemon & Chilli Marinade (p.113)	•				•			
Apricot & Herb Marinade (p.113)			•	•				
Chimichurri (p.113)	•	•			•			
South African Sosatie (p.113)	•	•		•				
Herb Paste for Fish (p.114)					•			
Paste for Cooked Meats (p.114)		•	•	•				
Papaya Marinating Paste (p.114)		•	•					
Jamaican Jerk Paste (p.114)	•		•					
North African Spice Paste (p.115)	•			•				
Herb Rub (p.115)		•	•					•
Traditional Rib Rub (p.115)		•	•					

	Poultry	Beef	Pork	Lamb	Fish & shellfish	Vegetables	Salads	Pasta, rice & noodles
Indian Dry Rub (p.115)	•	•	•	•	•			
Apple Sauce (p.116)			•			•		
Cranberry Sauce (p.116)	•		•					
Gooseberry Sauce (p.118)					•			
Cherry Sauce (p.118)		•	•	•				
Plum Sauce (p.118)	•		•	•		•		
Fresh Berry Sauce (p.118)	•			•	•			
Cumberland Sauce (p.118)	•	•		•				
Cherry Cumberland Sauce (p.118)	•	•		•				
Mint Sauce (p.118)				•				
Bread Sauce (p.119)	•							
Horseradish Cream Sauce (p.119)	•	•	•					
Chrain (p.119)	•	•			•			
Pesto (p.120)	•					•	•	•
Dill Pesto (p.120)	•					•	•	•
Coriander Pesto (p.120)	•		•	•		•	•	•
Olive Pesto (p.120)	•					•	•	•
Tapenade (p.122)						•	•	
Anchoïade (p.122)						•	•	
Simple Salsa Verde (p.122)	•		•	•	•			•
Agrodolce (p.122)	•					•	•	
Skordalia (p.122)	•					•	•	
Romesco (p.123)	•			•		•		
Rouille (p.123)	•				•	•		
Tarator (p.124)	•					•		
Pistachio Tarator (p.124)	•					•		
Muhammra (p.124)	•					•		
Malay Peanut Sauce (p.124)	•	•	•	•		•		
Hot Anchovy Butter (p.125)					•	•		
Hot Piri-Piri Butter (p.125)	•				•	•		
Tamarind Dipping Sauce (p.125)	•				•	•		
Chinese Dipping Sauce (p.125)	•				•	•		
Thai Dipping Sauce (p.125)	•	•	•	•	•	•		
Vietnamese Dipping Sauce (p.125)	•	•	•	•	•	•		

DESSERT SAUCES

	Ice-cream	Fruit	Tarts	Steamed puddings	Pancakes
Crème Anglaise (p.126)	•	•	•	•	
Chocolate Custard (p.126)	•	•	•	•	
Brandy Custard (p.126)	•	•	•	•	
Berry Custard (p.126)	•	•	•	•	
Honey Custard (p.126)	•	•	•	•	•
Caramel Custard (p.126)	•	•	•	•	
Sugar Syrup (p.128)	•	•	•	•	•
Zabaglione (p.128)		•	•		
Blueberry Zabaglione (p.128)		•	•		
Mango Zabaglione (p.128)		•	•		•
Yogurt & Honey Sauce (p.128)		•	•		•
Banana Caramel Sauce (p.129)	•				
Pineapple & Ginger Sauce (p.129)	•		•		•
Raisin Sauce (p.129)	•			•	
Orange & Red Wine Sauce (p.130)			•		
Passion Fruit Sauce (p.130)	•	•			
Maple Pecan Sauce (p.130)	•			•	•
Cooked Fruit Coulis (p.130)	•	•	•	•	
Fresh Fruit Coulis (p.130)	•	•	•		
Simple Chocolate Sauce (p.132)	•	•		•	•
White Chocolate Sauce (p.132)		•			
Fudge Sauce (p.132)	•				•
Rich Fudge Sauce (p.132)	•		•		•
Nut Fudge Sauce (p.132)	•		•		•
Ginger Fudge Sauce (p.132)	•		•		
Brandy Fudge Sauce (p.132)	•				
Brandy Butter (p.133)			•	•	•
Rum & Ginger Butter (p.133)			•	•	•
Orange Butter (p.133)			•	•	•
Cherry Butter (p.133)			•	•	•

INDEX

Bold page numbers indicate
a complete recipe; *italics* refer
to pages with illustrations

ACKNOWLEDGMENTS

Author's Appreciation
Writing a book such as *Sauces & Salsas* is a team effort and I would like to thank all who were involved in its creation. In the office: to Susannah Marriott who always has time for my moans but allows me the freedom (wherever possible) to express myself; to Tracey Ward, and to Nicky Graimes who, although did not work on the book, was involved in the original concept. Thanks go to my assistant Alison Austin who always stays calm; to Amanda Young, my angel, who inspired many of the Southeast Asian sauces; to Sue Storey, Jane Suthering and Jane Middleton. Special thanks must go to Ian O'Leary whose unfailing patience, strong sense of humour and superb artistry brought life and vitality to the book, and to his assistant Emma Brogi; and finally to my editor Nasim Mawji whose enthusiasm, friendship, inquiring mind and intelligence made this book such a pleasure to write.

Dorling Kindersley would like to thank David Summers and Janice Anderson for editorial work; Bodum for the supply of pots and pans; Celia Morris at Kitchen Aid for supplying an electric mixer; The Fresh Olive Company for supplying olive oil; Pam Bewley at Magimix for supplying a Magimix; Hujo's restaurant in Berwick Street. Thanks to Valerie Chandler for the index.